Revolutionary
War in World
Strategy

Robert Thompson

Formerly Head of the British
Advisory Mission in Vietnam

Revolutionary War in World Strategy 1945-1969

TAPLINGER PUBLISHING COMPANY
NEW YORK

First published in the United States in 1970 by
Taplinger Publishing Co., Inc.
New York, New York

ISBN 0–8008–6785–8

Library of Congress Catalog Card Number 72–116546

Printed in Great Britain

This book is dedicated to the peasants of Thanh Hoa and Nghe An Provinces in North Vietnam who in 1956, without any hope of outside support, rebelled against tyranny imposed as a result of revolutionary war.

Contents

Author's Note

IN TWO previous books, *Defeating Communist Insurgency* and *No Exit from Vietnam*, I have dealt with the practical aspects of communist insurgency and counter-insurgency on the ground and with the strategy and counter-strategy of revolutionary war within the context of the Vietnam war. Inevitably it has been necessary to repeat certain points in these two books to explain revolutionary war and its techniques, but this book is intended as the final one in a trilogy to show how revolutionary war has been used as an instrument of policy in the world strategy of Russia and China during the last twenty-five years.

I am very grateful to a former colleague, Dennis J. Duncanson, for much good advice, and to Mrs Deborah Robinson for so patiently typing the drafts and the text.

R.T.

Winsford,
Somerset.
8 October, 1969.

Foreword

AT A moment in world history when the United States is deploying all its resources of knowledge about prospects for bringing the bitter war in Vietnam to an end, this book, third and last in a trilogy (the earlier two books were *Defeating Communist Insurgency* and *No Exit from Vietnam* by the same author, Sir Robert Thompson, former head of the British Advisory Mission to Vietnam), brings welcome clarification of tangled events, and skillfully helps outsiders both to comprehend the crises of today and to speculate with greater perspicacity about future developments.

Sir Robert makes his own view of the Vietnam tragedy immediately clear when he dedicates his book "to the peasants of Thanh Hoa and Nghe An Provinces in North Vietnam who in 1956, without any hope of outside support, rebelled against tyranny imposed as a result of revolutionary war."

The author points out at the start that this book is intended as the final volume in a trilogy to show how revolutionary war has been used as an instrument of policy in the world strategy of Russia and China during the last twenty-five years. In his opinion, for the past quarter of a century, Moscow's two policy aims —Communist domination of the world and defense of the Soviet base at home—have remained constant. "Its strategy," he asserts, "has been flexible and its instruments of policy, of which revolutionary war, is one, have been varied." And, looking to the future, he asserts that "It would be safe to assume that there will be no change during the 1970's, although the pattern of conflict itself may alter."

He contends that "There is every indication that Russia is now moving from the position of being a

super-nuclear power into one of being a global power."
This development, however, could not have come as a
surprise to so keen an observer of world affairs as Sir
Robert, since Russia, which had already been a great
—if not always a militarily strong—empire under
both Tsars and Commissars, could have been expected
to assert its interests not only in Europe and Asia,
since it forms part of both those continents, but also
in other areas of the world, as Britain and France had
done in their day, and the United States has been
doing since World War II.

This is not surprising. The same policy would have
been followed by the Tsarist Empire had there never
been a Communist revolution. But in Southeast Asia,
as Sir Robert rightly points out, the role Moscow plays
is doubly important for the future of the U.S.S.R. For,
unlike Britain and France in their heyday, and the
United States today, the U.S.S.R. must operate on
two far-flung fronts of its vast domain—both in
Europe and in Asia. Like other imperial powers of the
past, the Communist empire must face the complex
problems, not merely of subjugating other nations,
but, far more difficult, of winning their support on
both political and economic planes if it is to retain the
role of leadership it has vigorously sought outside its
borders, but does not always find it easy to command.

In developing this thesis, Sir Robert gives a penetrating and convincing analysis of the role the U.S.S.R.
is now playing on the world scene, both in terms of its
successes and of the problems it has had to face in the
past and may be expected to face in the future.

VERA MICHELES DEAN

1

Revolutionary War

IN THE twenty-five years between 1945 and 1969, from the end of World War II to the closing stages of the Vietnam war, the promotion and support of revolutionary war appear to have been an important aspect of both Russian and Chinese foreign policy. Throughout the world, beginning with Greece in 1945, there has been an unending succession of such wars in Asia, Africa and Latin America and some of them still continue at varying degrees of intensity. New outbreaks of violence are frequently occurring many of which bear some relation to revolutionary war, while in others its techniques have been imitated or its theory followed.

In a famous and well reported speech at Montreal on 18 May, 1966, Mr Robert S. McNamara, then the United States Secretary of Defence, stated that, at the beginning of 1958, there were twenty-three prolonged insurgencies still going on in the world and that, on 1 February, 1966, there were forty. Excluding such wars as the Korean war, the war between Pakistan and India, the Israeli-Arab war and the Sino-Indian border war in the Himalayas, all of which were conventional in form, most of the other conflicts earned at the time a great variety of titles: partisan warfare, guerrilla warfare, brush-fire war, civil war, rebellion and insurgency. For a period the more popular title of the type of war with which we are concerned was "insurgency" or "communist insurgency" (hence the term "counter-insurgency" to describe the defence against it) but the more accepted title is now "revolutionary war".

In his speech Mr McNamara quite rightly pointed out that it would be "a gross over-simplification to regard communism as the central factor" in all the conflicts which have taken place throughout the under-developed world. Out of the 149 serious outbreaks of violence between 1958 and 1966 communists were involved in only fifty-eight and in seven of those they were themselves the target of the uprisings. It is, however, possible to wage a revolutionary war without direct communist sponsorship or involvement. In fact revolutionary war, in the sense in which we are dealing with it in this book, can be broadly divided into three types: those carried out under the leadership of the communist party, as in the two Vietnam wars; those which after victory resulted in the communist party gaining the leadership, as in Cuba (where Fidel Castro did not openly declare that he was a Marxist until he had won); and those in which any communist involvement is denied or even opposed but which may in the end advance the communist cause, as in Algeria.

Putting aside for the moment the extent of communist involvement in any particular revolutionary war, it is, however, to avowed communists that we must look for the main characteristics of this new form of war: to Marx for the original concept of struggle, to Lenin for the party organisation, to Mao Tse-tung for its application to a peasant society, to his heir-apparent Marshal Lin Piao for its application to world revolution, to Truong Chinh and General Vo Nguyen Giap for the refinement of its techniques in Vietnam and to Che Guevara for its spiritual appeal to the intellectual youth of the West. These were its inventors, its exponents, its prophets and its chief practitioners. It should not be surprising, therefore, to find that revolutionary war, as preached by well-known communists profiting originally from their experience in World War II, has been used subsequently as an instrument of Russian and Chinese foreign policy in order to spread communist influence and control and to encourage world revolution. But the question remains whether the promotion of revolutionary wars has been part of a consistent policy or to what extent such wars are partly a natural symptom of our times. An analysis must also be made of their effectiveness as a means of spreading communist influence and control in a period which has seen a continuous struggle between East and West and between communism and democracy.

Revolutionary war has not been the only instrument for the purpose of extending communist control, as Russia herself has recognised. For Russia in the immediate post-war years the Russian Army, or even a satellite army (North Korea), united front tactics (a temporary political alliance with non-communist parties, later to be discarded), and, in the post-Stalin era, trade and aid all had their parts to play, often more effectively than revolutionary war, but with the choice of instrument depending on circumstances rather than preference. For China, however, during the last ten years revolutionary war has been acclaimed as the paramount instrument, with Mao Tse-tung maintaining that the communist party must be in the vanguard and in control of every revolutionary movement. This difference of approach is one cause of the split between Russia and China and stems from the tendency, as between support for communist ideological doctrines and concern for national interest, of China to incline to the former and Russia to the latter.

It will be interesting to see that this has led to a situation where there have been, during the last twenty-five years, almost two distinct waves of revolutionary wars with Russia promoting and supporting the first and China the second. Before dealing with these in later chapters and showing how revolutionary war has been used as an instrument of policy in world strategy, it is first necessary to define it and describe its main features.

The best definition of revolutionary war, well suited to the Chinese approach, is: A form of warfare which enables a small ruthless minority to gain control by force over the people of a country and thereby to seize power by violent and unconstitutional means. The small ruthless minority has normally been the local communist party, but, of course, the techniques of revolutionary war could be used by a nationalist, socialist, racialist or fascist party with a similar organisation in much the same way. Naturally the larger the minority in the first instance (even possibly a majority in some cases), the quicker will victory be achieved. In all the best examples of revolutionary war, except Algeria, during the last twenty-five years the party has been the communist party and has initially represented only a small percentage of the people of the country concerned.

Revolutionary war, in its modern form, is easier to describe through its main features than it is to define. It is a war in three distinct phases. The first phase is defensive in character while the party's organisation within the population of the country is being built up.

This process can take a very long time, depending to a large extent on the attraction of the party's appeal to all sections of the population and on the efficiency and vigilance of the existing government. The second phase, after an adequate underground organisation has been developed, is a period of guerrilla warfare starting at a very low tempo but gradually rising in scale. This is designed, first, to expand the underground organisation and its control over the population at the expense of the government, secondly, to create regular military units of battalion size or larger and, thirdly, to neutralise the effectiveness of the government's armed forces, thereby rendering them powerless to save the state. When a point of equilibrium with the government has been reached, in effectiveness rather than numbers, then in the third phase the whole revolutionary movement goes over to the offensive and is prepared to engage in more open warfare until the government collapses and victory is won.

In revolutionary war the aim is always political. As Mao has stated: "Politics is war without bloodshed; war is politics with bloodshed." It is the aim of a communist party within a country to seize power and to effect a complete change in its system of government and in its social structure. The party will not be interested in merely reforming the existing system and structure. There will, however, be circumstances where, in the first instance, the aim may have to be more limited by, for example, accepting as a step towards the ultimate aim a form of coalition government with other parties and a compromise on the changes which may be made in the structure. But the ultimate aim will remain and the struggle will continue until it is achieved. The party's aim in revolutionary war does not change; only the method, often when others have been tried and failed, is changed.

The aim of the communist party should not be confused with the cause on which it bases its appeal and builds up its organisation for revolutionary war. In the first place, if people are to be attracted, the appeal must be directed to their vital interests and be sufficiently broadly based to embrace most sections of the community. Few will be attracted to a cause which is blatantly designed to give power to the communist party. Without question, in the most successful revolutionary wars of the last twenty-five years, the strongest appeal has been nationalism and patriotism based either on resistance to a conquerer, for example the Germans or Japanese, or on the gaining of independence from a colonial power. Once the strength of the party has been built up on such a basic course, then subsidiary causes of a more specific political or economic nature (often only pretexts such as land reform) can be developed to appeal to particular sections within the community. When the war has entered the second guerrilla warfare phase, the original cause will become less and less relevant because the immediate concern of most people will be survival for themselves and their families and there will be an inclination to support the side which looks like winning. It is at this point that the party, as one means of hastening the collapse of government and the existing structure, will be better able to exploit all the contradictions which exist within any society. These may be political, social, economic, racial or religious. The tension of the war will itself exacerbate all of them and create others. As

Che Guevara wrote (but himself failed to achieve in Bolivia): "It is not necessary to wait for the fulfilment of all conditions for a revolution because the focus of insurrection can create them."

Quite the most vital feature of revolutionary war is its organisation. This is established in two parts. The first, and by far the most important, is the political underground organisation within the population in which cells are created, by a process described as "bead-stringing", throughout the country in all villages and towns with particular emphasis on the penetration of student and labour organisations. In addition to the continual expansion of the cell system, it is the function of these cells to carry out propaganda, sub-version, sabotage, assassination and other terrorist incidents but the main function of the underground organisation as a whole is to provide a support base for the second part of the organisation—the military guerrilla units. No army can be raised and maintained unless it has a home base on which it can rely for its supplies and recruits. The underground organisation forms this base for the guerrilla units. When these start operating in the second phase of revolutionary war there is, therefore, a two-pronged attack on the government and on the groups who support it, with the underground organisation responsible for political subversion and terror, and the guerrilla units for military operations. Both are closely co-ordinated and the military activity of the guerrilla units is designed to aid the underground organisation in expanding its control over the population. As this control expands, so does the base and, with it, the capacity to support larger and larger military units until equilibrium with the government is reached and the whole movement can go over to the offensive in the third final phase.

It is essential at this point to understand the relationship between the organisation, the cause and the three phases of a revolutionary war. In very few cases has the original cause, which enabled the underground organisation to be built up during the first phase, been the same cause as that adopted during the subsequent phases. For example, in Greece, in China and in Malaya, the initial cause, which had great attraction, was resistance to the German or Japanese invaders. The same was partly true of Vietnam, though the more effective cause was to be independence from France during the Vietminh war from 1946 to 1954. The organisation having been established on these original causes, the revolutionary wars which followed (including the present Vietnam war) were then fought for a different cause during the second and third phases. In all these cases it would have been difficult for the communist party, if not impossible, to have built up the organisation on the basis of the cause for which the wars were actually fought. In studying any revolutionary war, therefore, when it breaks out into guerrilla warfare at the beginning of the second phase, it is necessary to assess whether its organisation or its ostensible cause (often no more than a pretext) is the vital factor because this will dictate the emphasis of the response. If the organisation is the vital factor, then the revolutionary movement will not be defeated by reforms designed to eliminate the cause. It will only be defeated by establishing a superior organisation and applying measures designed to break the revolutionary organisation.

This is important when considering the position of the individual in a threatened society. His actions, as every Marxist-Leninist understands, will be conditioned by his environment. He will have been attracted during the first phase by the original cause, but in the second phase with a new cause of much less attraction, he will be most influenced by the efficiency of the revolutionary organisation and the tensions which revolutionary war creates. He will not therefore be greatly influenced by a government merely offering reforms in response to a cause which has little attraction for him. When, however, a cause, such as nationalism, is consistent all the way through (as in Algeria), then it may be a more vital factor than the revolutionary organisation, in which case it is the political solution which must dominate the response. Generally it can be said that, where both the cause and the organisation are good, the revolutionary movement will win, probably at an early stage. The long-drawn-out struggle occurs when the organisation is good and the cause is weak. In this circumstance only through the strategy of protracted war can a revolutionary movement achieve victory.

The military strategy of revolutionary war on the ground has been well described by Mao Tse-tung as "using the villages to encircle the towns". This means that control is first gained over the population in the remoter villages and valleys on the fringe of inaccessible jungle, mountains or swamp. The area is then expanded during the guerrilla warfare phase, frequently over a period of several years, until control (sufficient to command recruits, supplies and petty services from the population) is gained over wide populated rural areas so that the towns, and the communications between them, are threatened. This will compel the government to disperse its forces to garrison the main centres and defend vital points thereby allowing the regular units of the insurgent to concentrate and attack them one by one in open battle until victory is achieved.

The higher political strategy of revolutionary war, however, is conceived in terms of time, space and cost. Time in the sense of patience is the key to this strategy. A communist party must be prepared to fight indefinitely with complete faith in the inevitability of final victory. The strength of its movement is forged by continual combat whereas the strength of a government is steadily eroded as its efforts to cope with the situation appear more and more futile. Mao described this forging process in the phrase: "A distant journey tests the strength of a horse and a long task proves the character of a man." Time also provides the opportunity either to exploit favourable tendencies in the internal or external situation or to consolidate (or even take one step backward) when trends are unfavourable.

If time is to be gained then space must be held. The term "space" is not used here in the sense of territory, as in positional warfare, but in the sense that the members of the political underground organisation and the guerrilla units must have freedom of movement throughout the whole country so that the government is threatened everywhere and, secondly, in the sense that the political underground organisation must penetrate all sections of society so that there are no sections on which the government can completely rely.

If space is to be held in this sense, it must be paid for in lives. This means that the whole organisation must function so efficiently that its expenditure in manpower is more than met by its ability to recruit replacements. The numerical force strength must steadily increase if the momentum of revolutionary war is to be maintained. A steady increase of strength can of course be more easily ensured when additional manpower can be infiltrated into the country. In most cases outside support has been confined to the training of indigenous people and to the supply of materials and arms. As will be seen, one case in which there has been massive outside support by way of additional manpower, has been Vietnam, particularly in the period from 1965 onwards. Naturally any form of outside support gives an enormous boost to the momentum and offensive potential of an insurgency within a country.

If a revolutionary war goes through all three phases, final victory can be achieved militarily when the regular forces of the insurgent defeat the government forces in conventional battle. This would be a classical ending in accordance with the orthodox theory. There are, however, other possible channels to victory. If the revolutionary cause is attractive to a majority of the people and the organisation is strongly established, victory can be achieved against a comparatively weak and inefficient government in the first or second phase through the collapse of that government. In most cases, however, the cause is not sufficiently attractive for this purpose. *This is the whole point of revolutionary war—that, by using its techniques, a small ruthless minority lacking a good cause and genuine popular support can succeed in overthrowing a government.*

Even in the third phase a conventional military victory is not an essential ending. If a revolutionary movement can maintain a high scale of operations at a cost, mainly in manpower, which is indefinitely acceptable to itself and can impose on the government, and any other power supporting it, costs which are not indefinitely acceptable to them, then in the end it must win. In this case the war becomes a contest of will rather than a trial of strength. The erosion of will can be accelerated and dissent amplified by the manoeuvre known as "fighting while negotiating", because the mere opening of negotiations, suggesting as it does a prospect of peace, automatically reduces the will of the defence to continue fighting. To a certain extent the guerrilla's morale is affected too, but his leaders are in a position to exhort him to continue fighting "unremittingly" in a "heightened struggle",* whereas the opposing leaders cannot issue such an appeal without being accused of prejudicing negotiations.

Certain types of terrain are obviously more suitable for a form of war which militarily uses the tactics and strategy of guerrilla warfare. It is essential for guerrilla units to achieve surprise and to be able to concentrate rapidly for attacks on weaker government forces and isolated outposts, while being able to disperse and disappear as soon as they are faced by stronger government forces (thereby enhancing, strangely enough, rather than diminishing their reputation for gallantry). This pattern of operations was described by Mao Tse-

* The "sacred appeal" of Ho Chi Minh, see "Two Vietnams or One" by Dennis J. Duncanson, in *The World Today* (Chatham House) of September 1969, p. 412.

tung in the phrase: "The strategy of guerrilla warfare is to pit one man against ten but the tactics are to pit ten men against one." Areas, therefore, which provide natural protection and cover in the form of jungle, mountain or swamp are the most suitable. This applies to most of Asia, Africa and Latin America. Clearly desert is the least suitable because with its lack of cover (and water) it can be dominated by government forces using aircraft, helicopters, armoured cars and electronic gadgetry. The terrain advantage is greatly improved if there is a lack of land communications so that the movement of government forces on the ground is restricted and easily observed. This also means that the few vital communication arteries, which the government must keep open, will themselves be vulnerable to guerrilla attacks, thus requiring a large proportion of the government forces to be deployed in a static role for their defence.

The word "terrain" is also frequently used to describe the political and economic situation within a country which exposes it to the dangers of revolutionary war. If there is political instability (or even just uncertainty, as after independence), administrative inefficiency and chronic insecurity, with law and order barely maintained, a country will be a ripe target for attack because, under these conditions (which can of course be promoted by a communist party over a period of time, as in West Bengal), the government cause and organisation will be weak and the revolutionary cause and organisation relatively strong. During revolutionary war, and in particular during the second phase of guerrilla warfare, the advantage will go to the side whose organisation is most effective in securing and exploiting the resources of the country. It should be understood in this respect that a revolutionary movement requires only a fraction of these, as compared with a government, to maintain itself and expand.

In his Montreal speech, Mr McNamara also drew attention to the connection between poverty and violence. He noted that, among the thirty-eight nations classified as very poor (with a per capita income of less than $100 a year), thirty-two had suffered violent conflict, frequently of long duration. Not in every case has the form of conflict been revolutionary war. In revolutionary war poverty can operate both ways. While it may sometimes be a cause,* it does at the same time make it almost impossible for such a war to be conducted effectively at a sufficient intensity. Generally speaking, revolutionary war tends to take place in agricultural communities where there is no great poverty but where there may be other types of exploitable grievance. Revolutionary war can only be carried on at a high tempo in a country which is comparatively well populated and developed and where there is a surplus both of energy and of resources. (If this surplus is denied to the government and harvested by the revolutionary forces, the latter gain a double advantage.) Revolutionary war is, therefore, less likely to occur, either in rich and densely populated countries or, at the other extreme, in open desert

* More research is required on this point, starting from de Tocqueville's finding that the French peasant in 1789 revolted against the *ancien régime* in those areas where social progress had been most marked and supported it where there had been no progress.

countries with a scattered population living in abject poverty.

There is one other essential ingredient for the successful conduct of this type of war. The people of a country must be physically and temperamentally fitted for it. A population which is suffering from an endemic disease or a debilitating complaint, e.g. malaria or liver fluke, will lack the strength and energy for great feats of physical and mental endurance. A fatalistic outlook will help to render members of a revolutionary movement less averse to danger and more indifferent to the sufferings of others. A tradition of violence and a measure of education will throw up the dynamic and imaginative leadership required. A striking example of these different attributes, quite apart from other social factors, can be found in Indo-China as between the energetic hard-working Viet-namese and the placid happy-go-lucky Laos.

It will be seen, therefore, that there are many features of revolutionary war which differentiate it from other forms of warfare and violent conflict and which entitle it to be classified as a separate, if not an entirely new, form of war. Because its aim is the take-over of a country by a revolutionary party and the complete destruction of the existing system of govern-ment and social structure, it bears no comparison with, for example, a *coup d'état* which replaces one ruling group by another, without destroying the existing structure, although there may be the intention to introduce changes and reforms. Nor does revolutionary war compare with a rebellion which has a more limited purpose such as to redress the wrongs of one particular group within the community. In this respect, for example, the secession of Biafra from Nigeria is a rebellion and bears no resemblance to revolutionary war, although guerrilla tactics may be used. The use of the military tactics and strategy of guerrilla warfare is, however, a major difference between revolutionary war and conventional war. There are also no front lines and no battles of any size, except possibly in the final stages. Another striking difference between revolutionary war and conventional war is that the base of the revolutionary movement within the population is in the forefront of the battle, well in advance of the guerrilla units, eating its way into the foundations of the government structure, whereas in conventional warfare the home base is in the rear and, other than as a source of supply, plays little part in offensive operations. Furthermore, in revolutionary war the revolutionary party seeks to gain control over the population first before it can defeat the opposing military forces, whereas in conventional warfare (even a civil war fought by conventional armies) this is the other way round.

But, in the popular mind, revolutionary war is most confused with guerrilla or partisan warfare. Here the main difference is that guerrilla warfare is designed merely to harass and distract the enemy so that the regular forces can reach a decision in conventional battles. However great their contribution to victory may be, guerrilla forces are not in a position to achieve it alone. There have been many examples of this, notably the Spanish guerrillas in the Peninsular War where the French armies were finally defeated in conventional battle by the Duke of Wellington, and in World War I where Colonel T. E. Lawrence in the

Arabian desert made a significant contribution to General Allenby's defeat of the Turkish armies in Palestine. Much the same was true of the many resistance movements in Europe and the Balkans during World War II, but the main German armies had to be decisively defeated in conventional battle before the war was won. Revolutionary war on the other hand is designed to reach a decisive result on its own. This decisive result is the attainment of the political aim (i.e. the take-over of a country) for which a military victory in the conventional sense may not be necessary.

There are other minor differences between revolutionary war and guerrilla warfare. In most examples guerrilla forces are conducting a resistance against a conqueror. Their aim is to help evict him and to restore the status quo. They are, therefore, by nature conservative and traditional rather than revolutionary, although, as we shall see, the respectability and glamour of resistance can be used by a communist party as a pretext in the process of building up its underground organisation. Rarely also can a guerrilla resistance movement afford the casualties incurred in a revolutionary war, partly because it lacks the organisation to replace them and the discipline to accept them. An ordinary guerrilla movement would tend to break up and wither away if its casualties were too heavy.

There are equally differences from the government point of view, not least of which is that in conventional war the soldiers win the war first and the politicians try to clear up the mess afterwards. In revolutionary war it is essential for a government to clear up the mess (and preferably not to make it) as the war goes on and to eliminate as far as possible the contradictions and dissensions within society. Clearing up the mess and eliminating the contradictions are, in revolutionary war, part of the war and not part of the subsequent peace.

There are obviously some serious weaknesses in revolutionary war which have to be overcome during the course of the struggle. Governments, particularly those supported by a Western power, have at their disposal much greater resources in the industrial, economic and military fields. These cannot be matched by the insurgent with his political cadres and armed propaganda units. The insurgent must first evade and then neutralise the superior strength of the government until his own forces have been built up to the point of equilibrium. In order to do this the revolutionary movement has to substitute subversion for weapons, feet for mechanical transport, men for machines, and must achieve human and political rather than industrial mobilisation. Victory obtained in this way also has an enhanced psychological effect by demonstrating that men and ideas are still superior to all the machines and gadgets of the scientific and technological age.

Even in favourable "terrain" the build-up phase, requiring as it does subversion and penetration, takes a great deal of time if the security of the budding organisation is to be preserved. Moreover, during this phase and the first part of the guerrilla war phase, the insurgent is logistically weak particularly in weapons. Many of these will be obsolete, or even home-made, until more modern weapons can be captured from the government and, in the final stages, an outside supply line (like the Ho Chi Minh trail) can be organised. All this means that the insurgents can never hope to deliver a single decisive blow. This point was recognised by Lenin when he said: "The uprising cannot assume the traditional form of a single blow, limited to a very short time and a very small area." The war must be protracted and spread, which was part of the theory developed by Mao.

Another weakness is that control of the population depends on the efficiency of the underground organisation, sometimes referred to as the "infrastructure", and on methods which include intimidation and terror. If the infrastructure is damaged or broken by government action, the whole movement will lose momentum and begin to collapse. Guerrilla units, dependent on the infrastructure for their daily needs and for recruits, will be forced to cease offensive operations and to forage instead. This will soon cause them to disperse and break up, thereby making their gradual elimination comparatively easy for the government. Intimidation and terror, if used by them too harshly and indiscriminately, may back-fire and rally all the uncommitted sections of the population to the government. In both these respects, however, the revolutionary movement does have an advantage over the government. Its infrastructure is invisible whereas the superstructure of the government organisation is not. Any damage done to the former, provided that it can be repaired, has few outwardly harmful psychological repercussions, whereas any damage done to the government's superstructure is highly visible and has an immediate effect. Similarly, with acts of terror, these are frequently unreported by terrified neighbours and are certainly screened from the television camera, whereas every action of the government, including accidents, is part of the news of the day and receives the widest publicity.

When a revolutionary movement becomes dependent for part of its resources and manpower on outside supply, there is always the risk that this may be cut off. While multiple supply lines through jungle and mountainous country are almost immune to military and air interdiction, those through open country or by sea are not. Circumstances may also arise where the supplier, for reasons of national interest, which could include international condemnation, may cease to support the insurgent. While a revolutionary movement can operate successfully without any outside supply, once it has come to rely on such support then a sudden cut-off may be disastrous to its operations and morale.

Finally, there is also the risk that the threatened government may adopt an intelligent policy and the correct counter-strategy, and show as much patience and determination as the insurgent. In these circumstances all the other weaknesses of a revolutionary movement already enumerated can be fully exploited and lead to its defeat.

From the experience of the last twenty-five years, this last risk seems to be the remotest of them all. There are many dilemmas facing a government which reduce its capacity to cope with revolutionary war. At the first signs of an incipient insurgency, and even more as the threat develops, in either colonial or independent under-developed territories, no one likes to admit that anything is going wrong. This automatically leads to a situation where government counter-measures are always too little and too late until the time comes when really drastic action has to be taken. Two further errors will then follow: the military forces of the government will be given *carte blanche* to go blundering round the countryside creating more insurgents than they catch or kill, and extremely repressive measures against the population as a whole will be introduced, most of which can be neither fairly nor effectively enforced. There are essential security measures, which are appropriate and effective during each phase of revolutionary war, but to introduce these at an early stage requires an awareness and knowledge of the threat for which the government's intelligence organisation may be caught unprepared. Moreover, the minimum security measures required at an early stage may still lead to accusations that the government is being repressive, because there is likely to be little evidence to prove the need for remedial action. By the time there is plenty of evidence these security measures, if imposed too late, will be inadequate and harsher measures will be required. By this time the government will have a full-scale revolutionary war, well into the guerrilla warfare phase, on its hands.

From the point of view of the insurgent, revolutionary war is total war. Every available weapon can be used against any target. There is no concern for, as Mao said, "stupid scruples about benevolence, righteousness and morality in war". These, however, are virtues which a government cannot lightly discard. In that sense, therefore, a government faced with total war is fighting a limited war. For a communist insurgent no holds are barred, not even the liquidation before or after victory of whole sections of the population, because for him the end justifies the means. He does not have to be judged by world opinion because victory will remove the whole country behind the iron curtain. But a government has to live with what it does and stand before the world in the full light of day.

In addition, governments which are seeking a place for their country in the modern world face many problems other than the threat of revolutionary war. Two of their chief concerns are development and modernisation, which are bound to some extent to upset the traditional pattern of society and to create tensions. These in turn can be exploited by the communist party, in Walt W. Rostow's words, "as scavengers of the modernisation process". But, by completely hampering development and modernisation for many years, revolutionary war can so retard progress that despair and disillusionment may in the end produce victory. It is partly for that reason that governments coping with revolutionary war are inclined to be impatient and frustrated. All their plans for the future may have to be postponed, and lost time becomes their greatest enemy. Newly independent countries are also frequently at a disadvantage compared with a colonial power. Apart from the superior resources immediately available to the latter, it is likely to have an experienced administrative organisation, capable of co-ordinating more efficiently all the complicated military and civilian measures required to produce an effective counter-strategy.

Another problem with which many new nations are

obsessed is that of maintaining unity. This can be threatened, as for example in India, Malaysia and Nigeria, by religious or racial divisions, or in other countries, for example Burma and Thailand, by the presence of ethnic minorities, particularly in remote border provinces. Colonial powers have frequently been accused of maintaining their position by a policy of "divide and rule". The point was that colonial powers, because their officials were neutral, could rule a country suffering from these divisions and weld it into a single nation. When the colonial power departed so did the impartiality, leaving a situation which others could exploit through a policy of "divide and destroy". The problem of maintaining unity has so occupied the governments of many countries that it has only been met at the expense of political and economic progress.

Most countries threatened by revolutionary war have been compelled to turn to the West for assistance; but in the West there has been a reluctance to study or understand the strategy and techniques of revolutionary war. A French writer has maintained that, because conventional armies and professional soldiers have rarely succeeded in defeating guerrilla movements of any size in the past, there has been a tendency for Generals (and staff colleges) to minimise the role of guerrilla operations as one way of concealing their own impotence, and that, in this, the Generals have been abetted by the military historians. For example, in spite of the American post-war involvement in China and the victory of the communists there in 1949, the works of Mao Tse-tung were hardly studied in the United States until English translations became available more than five years later. Yet, with the post-war eclipse of the colonial powers and the collapse of *Pax Britannica*, it was to the United States that most small countries would naturally look for assistance in combating revolutionary war.

Generals were not alone in failing to comprehend what they were up against. A large portion of the intellectual community in the West, and in particular in the United States, was even further behind them in failing to grasp the nature of revolutionary war and the reality of the situation within the countries threatened by it. It was almost as if there had been a conspiracy (and, in so far as the academic world has been penetrated by communists and fellow-travellers, there has been) to misinterpret events and always to give the insurgent the benefit of the doubt and the threatened government never. The two favourite themes of such misguided people have been either that revolutionary war represents a spontaneous uprising of the people, with which the communist party is only vaguely or indirectly connected, against a repressive, inefficient and corrupt government, or that it is the government and the Western power supporting it which has provoked an insurgent reaction and so started, or prolonged, the war.

Accusations of repression, inefficiency or corruption can be easily slung against most governments by those who are too arrogant to heed the beam in their own eye. The terms are in any case relative and to suggest that such failings can only be cured by revolution is contrary to historical experience. It can be said for such governments that they are not planning for their people what the communists will do if they win. Outside the communist bloc there is at least the chance of reform but we have witnessed what happens to those who attempt it within the bloc.

The two themes have led to the fatuous arguments that to oppose revolution is to go against the trend of history, and that intervention by a foreign nation even when invited by a threatened government is more likely to assist rather than contain the spread of communist influence. Words also have been so misused that they have lost their original meaning. The term "progressive", for example, is now applied solely to those who prefer violence and destruction to stability and construction. Double talk and double standards are employed in argument. A terrorist can disembowel a pregnant woman but a government cannot detain a suspect without trial. All this has helped to confuse public opinion in the West where attitudes have already been conditioned by ideas of conciliation, compromise and negotiation as the means of settling disputes. This makes it difficult to understand a form of war which is bitter and total and in which one side or the other must win before the struggle ends. The issue in revolutionary war is not one of partition of territory, or of a share in the government, or of a more equitable distribution of wealth and land, all of which might be negotiable. It is a struggle for power and a question of who will control the future destiny of the country concerned.

2

Russian Foreign Policy

SINCE 1917 Russian foreign policy has been dictated by two basic aims, the domination of the world through revolution and through the rise to power of communist parties in all countries, and the absolute necessity of defending the Soviet base. These traditional aims have equally governed the Soviet approach to foreign policy from 1945 right up to the present day. The first has always been regarded as a matter of seizing opportunities (which can be forecast and expected) while the second has been constant and overriding. Here can be seen the first beginnings of a split between the thrust of ideological doctrine and the pull of national interest.

Until the outbreak of World War II in 1939 little success was achieved with either aim. Although under the auspices of the Comintern communist parties existed and even thrived in many countries, not one succeeded in coming to power. In fact, a number, notably those in Germany, Italy and Japan, were destroyed by the fascist powers and Russia could do nothing to save them. The colonial territories of the great powers, and other areas already mentioned as suitable for revolutionary war, were an early target for communist penetration. In 1921 Stalin had stated: "If Europe and America may be called the front . . . the non-sovereign nations and colonies, with their raw materials, fuel, food and vast stores of human material, should be regarded as the rear, the reserve of imperialism. In order to win a war one must not only triumph at the front but also revolutionise the enemy's rear, his reserves." It has remained one of the strongest communist beliefs that the "cities" of the western world can best be attacked through the "countryside" of Asia, Africa and Latin America. Yet communism made little headway in the pre-war years against the colonial powers, because communist parties had no chance to develop a good cause with any appeal to largely peasant agricultural communities, which were in any case at this time politically apathetic. There was a minor social or economic appeal to the small urban proletariat and to industrial workers, but the consequent strikes and unrest were short-lived and had little effect. The governments concerned had a keen awareness of the threat and their administrations, especially their intelligence organisations, were too efficient. Moreover, the colonial powers were able to accomplish a gradual political and economic improvement which did not undermine the existing social structure in their respective territories. There was scant cause for an uprising and certainly no base for a successful revolutionary war. Most minor conflicts or rebellions were also easily and cheaply dealt with by the colonial powers and in no way taxed their resources. It was the age when the gun-boat, the machine-gun, mountain artillery, aircraft and armoured cars were dominant. There was a long way to go before the art of revolutionary war was sufficiently developed, not only to take on technically and mechanically superior forces, but also to make such a war extremely expensive for the Western powers.

From the point of view of the defence of the Soviet base, Russia still suffered from the provisions of the Treaty of Brest-Litovsk which left the Russian southern front from Estonia to the Black Sea vulnerable to attack. This meant that the emphasis of Russia's defensive policy had to be concentrated on the industrialisation of the country, the collectivisation of its agriculture and the build-up of its military forces. No progress could be made in the extension of the southern front to a more defensible position nor was there any prospect of acquiring a "warm-water port", in keeping with traditional Russian policy over the previous centuries. There was even a grave risk that, as a Russian statesman in the eighteenth century had said: "That which stops growing begins to rot."

It was the need to extend her frontier, as part of an active defence policy, which accounted for the Russian invasion of Finland and her infernal alliance with the Nazis to carve up Poland in 1939. These events, which did the communist cause great harm throughout the world, were later more than offset by the heroic defence of the Russian people and the subsequent defeat of the German armies on their eastern front. By 1945 goodwill for Russia was fully restored and communist party prestige in other countries also recovered, as a result of the part it played in the many resistance movements, especially in France, Italy and Japanese-conquered territories in the Far East. The question was whether Russia would maintain her wartime co-operation with the West in the interests of future world order. But her new position seemed to those in the Kremlin to vindicate the teaching of Lenin and the views of Stalin himself. There were obviously great opportunities for expansion both in Europe and the Far East. In August, 1945, the Soviet President, Kalinin, predicted the Russian course: "Even now, after the greatest victory known to history, we cannot for one minute forget the basic fact that our country remains the one socialist State in the world."

The two basic themes of Russian foreign policy were, therefore, still uppermost. This clearly showed in the dispute which developed over the interpretation of the Yalta Agreement with regard to Poland. There were fundamental differences between Russia and the West in their approach to the problem. The Russian failure to support the Warsaw uprising, and the consequent destruction by the Germans of the nationalist and non-communist parties involved, were an ominous indication that Russia would regard the chaotic conditions in many countries as an opportunity, not for continued co-operation with the West, but for supporting the rise of communist parties to power. Stalin justified the Russian attitude to Poland by remarking to Churchill that the Soviet Union had the right to demand for Poland a regime that would be friendly toward Russia. He cynically pointed out that Russia in her turn would have no objection to any arrangement made by the British in the case of countries like Belgium or even Greece,* which could be regarded as within the British sphere of influence. The real divergence lay in the words "friendly toward" which after all has been the relationship between Britain and Belgium for a century. Russia interpreted these words to mean that she should be in full control and that under no circumstances could any of the governments of territories like Poland be given a chance to become "unfriendly toward" her. The doctrine of "limited sovereignty" had yet to be invented.†

It must be remembered that Russia still regarded all Western policy with great suspicion and that this was

* But see the next chapter for what happened there.
† The term was applied to Czechoslovakia in 1968.

endemic to the communist way of thought and view of events. Nothing the West could do would allay this—not even if the United States had presented Russia with a brand new atom bomb on a platter.

Furthermore, at the end of the war, Russia herself was physically devastated. This compelled her to remain isolated and to manufacture a hostile West as a means of gearing her people to the enormous task of restoring the economy. In that sense the war was not over for Russia and there could be no relaxation or liberalisation. It was not that Russia feared any Western aggressive intentions, although only the Americans had the bomb. The fact that she started to demobilise her armies was evidence of that. Her policy was dictated by the fear of an internal breakdown which made the restoring of the Soviet base the vital consideration. Domestically this required the revival of her economic and industrial strength but externally it also required the safeguarding of her frontiers. It must be remembered that Russia has three fronts, first and most important her southern or European front, second in importance her far eastern front facing China and Japan, and third her central front facing Turkey and Iran. From the defence point of view she had to avoid weakness or instability on the two major fronts simultaneously. One of them must always be stabilised and preferably both.

While this was Russia's chief post-war pre-occupation, the Western Powers were concentrating on their own post-war recovery and the demobilisation of their military forces. The new Labour Government in Britain was keen to establish a fresh relationship with Russia and was innocent enough to think that both countries were striving towards "the realisation of the world of the common man". The United States tended towards a policy which sought to maintain peace through the United Nations and a system of collective security in agreement with the Russians. If anything, the United States still seemed to regard British imperialism as more dangerous and sinister than any intention of Soviet expansion. There was, therefore, no question at this stage of Russian policy being influenced or provoked by Western initiative. There was, however, latent in the situation, the double danger for the West that collective security without agreement would render co-operation illusory, and that the Russian preference for dividing the world into spheres of influence would lead to confrontation when there was no understanding on the boundaries between the spheres. The first warning was given by Sir Winston Churchill in his "iron curtain" speech in March, 1946, at Fulton, Missouri. This speech was quite out of tune with public opinion in both Britain and the United States but it indicated to the Russians that their plans for expansion would have to be executed with some caution and counter-balanced with gestures of accommodation.

There were two new factors in the post-war situation which were to have their influence on revolutionary war—the invention of atomic weapons and the rise of nationalism. While there is no evidence that Russia ever feared a pre-emptive attack by the United States when the latter alone had the bomb, she did realise that she could not get into a position of direct confrontation at any point which was of vital interest to the United States. This same consideration continued to apply when both the super-powers had developed sophisticated nuclear weapons and means of delivery which acted as a mutual deterrent. The great problem for Russia was to decide when an area was of vital interest to the United States. For a long time the United States proved most unreliable in indicating when this was the case and frequently did it so late, partly because the very idea of spheres of influence was anathema to her statesmen, that confrontation became inevitable. *The great advantage of revolutionary war as an instrument of policy in the nuclear age was to be that it avoided direct confrontation.* Although the two super-powers might be ranged on opposing sides, revolutionary wars could safely be waged without fear of real escalation. For the communist powers, therefore, revolutionary war was a low-risk war.

This has remained the situation throughout the last twenty-five years while both the United States and Russia have had an "assured destruction capability", even after absorbing a surprise first strike. It is this capability which has been the deterrent, but only in a limited sense, because the capability of mutual destruction reduces the range of the types of aggression that can be deterred. For example, when America alone had the bomb, it did not deter Russia from putting great pressure on Berlin in 1948, nor from promoting the Korean war in 1950. The point has been very clearly made by Mr McNamara: "We and our allies will require substantial non-nuclear forces in order to cope with levels of aggression that massive strategic forces do not in fact deter. This has been a difficult lesson to learn." The difficult lesson for the public to learn, but well understood by both super-powers, was not that revolutionary war could not be deterred by nuclear weapons, but that there was very little risk of a revolutionary war leading directly to a nuclear war. For example, neither side has had any intention of (and has taken every step to avoid) getting into World War III over Vietnam.

The second new factor in the post-war situation was the rise of nationalism, particularly in the colonial territories of the European powers which had been overrun by or threatened by the Japanese. The days of colonialism were numbered and the peoples of the territories concerned had been rudely shaken out of their previous political apathy to seek not just independence and control over their own future destiny, but a place in a modern and developing world. Here was a great new force which could well affect the whole balance of power. Would it be aligned with East or West, or would it be neutral? The success of communist parties in many countries would depend on their relationship with the nationalist movements. As we shall see, where the communist party captured the nationalist movement it has been more successful in revolutionary war.

In support of revolutionary war as an instrument of policy both Russia as a communist state and the communist parties in many countries, apart from prestige and goodwill gained during the war, had further assets. The parties themselves had greatly increased their strength through the experience of resistance during the war within Europe and the territories conquered by the Japanese. In spite of the dissolution of the Comintern in 1943 in the interests of the war-time Alliance, it was still strictly to the central party in

Moscow to which all these world-wide communist parties looked for leadership. Their organisational weapon forged by Lenin was primed and loaded.

Lenin had early realised the need for "a militant organisation of agents" or, in other words, an army for political combat. But, whereas soldiers could be recruited by general conscription and controlled by legal powers and a measure of physical isolation, party members had to be selected and controlled by indoctrination and a measure of insulation from the community rather than isolation. A member who was voluntarily won over on ideological grounds had to be turned into an activist agent for seizing power. The indoctrination gave him a new moral and intellectual world which cut him off but did not remove him, as in a religious order, from the community. This helped to absorb him into the party, thereby increasing the insulation, which was further enhanced by the conspiratorial nature of the work, especially if it was illegal. It was not enough to rely merely on discipline, propaganda and the preaching of revolution. There had also to be continuous action through the systematic exploitation of every opportunity for gaining power in all social institutions and fields of activity. The action of this struggle for power became the dynamo of the party. Individual members could then be easily controlled through a hierarchical committee system providing a managerial structure of leadership. This leadership was co-opted, not elected in the democratic sense, and policy was decided through forms of self-criticism and discussion, which were never allowed to develop into criticism of the central party or of the leadership. Iron discipline and strict principles formed the basic strength of the organisation, but principles did not apply to the party's activities. These were entirely opportunistic whether legal or illegal. The control mechanisms eventually led to a situation where party members could be relied on both to think and act without direction. The dissolution of the Comintern, therefore, and in 1945 Ho Chi Minh's pretended dissolution of the Indo-China Communist Party, had no significant effect on the organisation. Both dissolutions were calculated only to deceive.

Given its organisational weapon the party, in order to seize power, must then do two things: gain control over the mass of the population and destroy, or at least neutralise, its competitors for power. Because it operates most actively deep within the community this gives it access to the mass target. In order to lead and mobilise the masses, the party must be identified with them by emphasising in its programme their interests without revealing its own motive of seizing power. The prospects are greatly improved if the party can operate legitimately and openly, but without prejudice to illegal underground activity. In this situation the united front technique will give the greatest access to the target power bases. Such a front, however, must be led by the party and there should be no compromise with any other political party or ideology just in order to advance the front. Other parties should be used instead to advance the interests of the communist party and supported where necessary as, in Lenin's words, "the rope supports a hanged man". The party's main enemies were, therefore, to be not so much the existing governments or regimes holding power but its

rivals for the power base, either other left-wing socialist parties or nationalist movements. If the united
front tactics worked, then the existing institutions and
structure of the state could be penetrated and gradually
captured but, if they did not, then the whole state and
social structure of the country would have to be destroyed. For this purpose revolutionary war became a
most effective instrument.

That the organisational weapon of the party could
be used to fight a new form of war using the strategy
and tactics of guerrilla warfare was one of the lessons
of World War II. The French *maquis* were reputed to
have been worth twelve divisions to the Allies and
Tito's partisans in Yugoslavia succeeded in tying down
thirty German divisions. Soviet partisans in the
German-occupied area of Russia are credited with
having killed 300,000 Germans, including 30 generals,
and to have derailed more than 3,000 trains. In one
night as many as 1,000 attacks on German communications were carried out. Initially, however, the German forces were often well received and welcomed by
the peasants in Russia, but partisan activity and the
mutilation of German prisoners soon provoked German
reactions against civilians which, in turn, created a
hostile population. There is no evidence that Russia
had prepared her people in advance for partisan warfare. The population were forced into the movement
by the German reaction, and soldiers cut off from their
units became partisans in preference to being prisoners.
At first there was no centralised control but this was
objectionable to the central party because independent
irregulars do not necessarily make good communists.
It became necessary to combine the organisational

weapon of the party with the strategy and tactics of partisan warfare.

This went beyond Lenin's concept of an armed struggle. Although he did not reject any combat method and preached that the various types of struggle must be analysed within their historical framework, to him the armed struggle had had the more limited objectives of assassinating individual officials and seizing money from the government and private sources to finance the revolution. He did, however, foresee that conditions would dictate the form of struggle, rising through the stages of strikes and demonstrations to general strikes, peasant uprisings and military uprisings. He also made the point, to those who complained that partisan warfare would disorganise the party and its work within the community, that the party must be in control. Whatever the form of conflict created by political and economic causes, the party had to take advantage of it. Whereas Lenin, and following him Stalin, accepted the need for war in a revolutionary struggle, it was Mao Tse-tung who was now reducing it to an art within the framework of communist ideology. The situation in China and the teaching of Mao was the final main asset available to Russia in the post-war situation.

To summarise, we have, therefore, the two basic aims of Russian foreign policy: communist domination of the world and the defence of the Soviet base. The instruments: the Soviet Army, the development of satellite armies, united front tactics, trade and aid, and finally revolutionary war. The assets: prestige, the organisational weapon of the communist party, the experience of resistance, and the new teaching of Mao

Tse-tung. And, lastly, the arenas: the three Russian fronts and the newly emerging countries.

Of the arenas the most important was always the European front and, in the immediate post-war years, the most important instrument was to be the Soviet Army. Revolutionary war, however, had a part to play both in Greece and in the Far East.

3

The Cold War

As STALIN was later to say: "The reason why there is now no Communist government in Paris is because in the circumstances of 1945 the Soviet Army was not able to reach French soil."[*]

This telling remark summarises Russian policy on her main front in the immediate post-war years. Estonia, Latvia and Lithuania just disappeared down the Soviet gullet. The Yalta Agreement, however, prevented Stalin from being quite so openly voracious in respect of the other territories on his frontier under Soviet military occupation. The rivals to the communist party in Poland having been betrayed in the Warsaw uprising and destroyed, Russia had no great problem in securing a communist government and Soviet political control. Communist parties were also hoisted into power by the Soviet Army in Rumania, Bulgaria and later East Germany. In Hungary, however, a free election did take place in November, 1945, and the communist party polled only 17 per cent of the votes. But, by 1948, thanks to the presence of the Soviet Army, the party was in full control of the government.

Czechoslovakia presented a different story and is of interest, from the point of view of revolutionary war, in showing what happens when there is a coalition government with a communist party—a favourite compromise proposal for a negotiated settlement (sic) of the war in Vietnam in 1968-9. After elections in 1946 the communist party held the Premiership and the Ministry of Interior in a coalition government with non-communist democratic parties. Two years'

[*] See J. M. Mackintosh, *Strategy and Tactics of Soviet Foreign Policy* (O.U.P., 1962), p. 15n.

experience of such a regime greatly reduced the popularity of the communist party and, in 1948, a crisis arose when the Minister of Interior replaced eight police chiefs in Prague by communists. He refused to cancel the appointments when instructed to do so by the Cabinet, whereupon some of the non-communist ministers offered to resign. The communist party immediately armed the workers' militia and organised demonstrations in the capital. The Soviet Deputy Foreign Minister (V. A. Zorin) suddenly arrived in Prague to supervise what followed. The communists, led by the Premier (Gottwald), by threatening civil war compelled the ailing President Benes to accept the resignations and to invite Gottwald to form a new government. Benes then resigned as President and died later that year. His colleague, the Foreign Minister Jan Masaryk, before his murder, was under duress and other non-communist leaders fled abroad. This opportunistic coup is a perfect example of what a ruthless minority in a coalition government can achieve even when its eclipse through democratic processes is imminent.

Another interesting case from the point of view of revolutionary war was that of Yugoslavia because it showed the first clash of interest between nationalism and communism. The Yugoslav Communist Party under Marshal Tito, having led the resistance during the war and ensured its accession to power by eliminating its rival monarchist party, was able to form a communist government as soon as the German armies retreated. The country could not be occupied by the Soviet Army because it was an ally and not a conquered territory. This prevented the Russians from importing a communist government of their own choice. None of the methods used to subjugate the other satellites could be so easily employed. Nevertheless, the tactics of trying to penetrate the police and security forces with Soviet officials and of controlling the country's economic life were tried. Attempts were also made to recruit agents within the Yugoslav administration for Soviet Intelligence and, conversely, the Yugoslavs were accused of not purging their ministries of spies, which was the usual Soviet method of securing the dismissal of unfriendly officials. Propaganda attacks were also made on the Yugoslav leaders. All this was resisted with pained surprise by the Yugoslav Communist Party. Industrial companies, which were meant to be formed by an equal provision of capital from the two countries under a Russian director, were wound up by the Yugoslavs when the Russians failed to put their money up but retained the direction. The real crunch came in 1948 when Stalin insisted on an economic and customs federation between Bulgaria and Yugoslavia which would have reduced the latter to satellite status. To Russia it was intolerable that a national communist party almost on her own frontier should adopt an independent policy. The federation was rejected by Yugoslavia and she was expelled from the bloc. This had its repercussions in other satellite states where communist leaders, who might have inclined to a similar independent line, were purged. It also had repercussions on the outcome of the revolutionary war being waged in Greece.

From the Soviet point of view Greece occupies a dominant strategic and geographical position, both providing access to the Eastern Mediterranean (the "warm-water port" policy) and forming a link between the southern and central Russian fronts. It was on this central front that the Russians had suffered their first major set-back after the war. During the war Russian forces had occupied the Iranian border province of Azerbaijan and established a communist regime there. Many factors, such as the presence of the Soviet Army, the proximity of the border and the feudal nature of the Iranian government, all seemed to be in Russia's favour. What is more, the United States had raised no real objection to her absorption of Eastern Europe so there seemed no reason why there should be any opposition to the seizure of such an unimportant and remote province in which America had no interest at all—other than a written agreement made at Yalta which had been quite specific about the withdrawal of Allied forces from Iran. The Russian attempt to stay there in support of its regime clearly violated the agreement and, although no United States interests were directly involved, the joint British and United States support for Iran at the United Nations secured a Russian withdrawal.

In an earlier political campaign against Turkey in the closing stages of the war, Russia, having denounced her treaty of friendship, had demanded the return of certain areas and proposed a joint responsibility for the defence of the Straits which would have involved the stationing of Soviet troops on the Bosphorus. Turkey, however, politically and financially supported by Britain, had stood firm. Later, in resisting the continued Russian claims, she was to be supported by the United States, already alerted by Azerbaijan and now about to be drawn further into the arena by the situation in Greece to which Russia had turned as a means of outflanking Turkey.

The strategic position of Greece made her an attractive target for the communists but, because the country lay outside the Soviet sphere of influence and out of reach of the Soviet Army, the only instrument of conquest available was revolutionary war. In this respect the terrain of Greece was ideal. Two-thirds of the country, including its frontier areas, was rocky and mountainous and contained only 40 per cent of its people, nearly all of whom were peasant farmers. Villages were widely separated and communications were poor. All this made it difficult for conventional forces to operate but ideal for guerrilla warfare.

By the end of 1943 the Greek Communist Party (KKE) had captured the resistance movement to the German occupation, and the People's Liberation Army (ELAS), which was the military arm of the KKE, controlled 20,000 guerrillas. A well-established underground organisation was operating and the subsidiary organisations of the KKE covered all aspects of Greek life. Arms were obtained from the defeated Greek Army, from Allied supply drops and, after the Allied armistice with Italy, from disarmed Italian occupation forces. Barbarous atrocities were committed against individual Greeks who refused to join the ranks of the National Liberation Front (EAM), on the ground that they were collaborators, so that no one could refuse to join. The better recruits, however, were former members of the Greek Army, but because they were regarded as unreliable by the communists, their units were always accompanied and controlled by political commissars of the KKE.

During the occupation, the object of the KKE was not to evict the Germans and restore national independence. Its real concern was to increase the strength of ELAS sufficiently to give the KKE complete control over the country. Its intention was not to help the Allies win the war but to help Moscow win the peace. Armed resistance to the Germans was the barest minimum necessary to camouflage the real purpose of the party. There were few operations against the German conquerors because they were not the political target of ELAS. The Germans did not even have to attack the ELAS mountain strongholds because they presented no threat to the occupying forces. The military objectives of ELAS were strictly related to the political aim and their main operations were therefore conducted against members of non-communist parties and, in October, 1944, against British and Greek units when they re-occupied the country. The KKE even did a deal with the Nazis for supplies of arms in return for not interfering with the German withdrawal. When the Allied commander ordered the ELAS forces to disband, they refused and launched an armed revolt. The KKE gave way and the Varkiza Agreement was signed in February, 1945. This represented only a tactical withdrawal by the communists and most of the ELAS forces took to the mountains while their leaders sought refuge in neighbouring, and by this time communist, States to await the departure of the British.

The Russians did not fail to notice that the British involvement in Greece in 1944 was not particularly

popular in the United States and was certainly unpopular with the Labour Party in Britain. With the
fall of Churchill they had every reason to expect that
they would get a free hand, although their action was
predictable and their motive was in line with past
foreign policy concepts. The United States had not
supported Britain in 1944 and, while there were still
some British troops present, there seemed no reason
why the United States would come in now to support
a government fighting communism in a civil war. After
all, where the stakes were very much greater in China
at this time, in the most important revolutionary war
of them all, the United States was still trying to
establish a coalition government between the nationalists and the communists.

Everything else was also in favour of the Russians.
The northern frontiers of Greece all bordered communist States, there was a guerrilla movement
operating on a large scale, and the other Greek political
parties were in the usual disarray. The Greek people
had suffered from all the ill-effects of an occupation
combined with a resistance movement. There had been
oppression, starvation, inflation and charges and
counter-charges of collaboration. There was complete
ideological and political confusion, with the result that
the KKE had been able to attract some support from
every section of the community, thereby gaining
"space".

By 1947 the ELAS forces had been increased to
23,000 with 8,000 in reserve and more in training over
the borders. The underground organisation of the KKE
was reputed to be 50,000 strong with about three-
quarters of a million supporters. The Greek Government

forces totalled about 182,000, but these were deployed in penny packets throughout the country in defence of towns and villages. Guerrilla activity up to this point was restricted to recruiting, the build-up of supplies, the sabotage of communications and general harassment. Over 700,000 people had already fled as refugees from the rural areas to the towns. The war was well into phase two and the initiative was entirely with the guerrilla forces.

The West was faced with the usual dilemma. Because of the requirement for "indisputable proof of guilt", there was the usual tendency to appease on the ground that communist activity might have been provoked by government excesses. There was a very grave danger that the psychological success of the communists would soon lead to material gains and that, because the hot aspects of the war were being played down and the cold aspects played up, the war would be lost before it was fought. The Russians, however, had misjudged the American reaction. The situation in Greece brought President Truman down to Congress to announce: "It must be the policy of the United States to support free peoples who are resisting attempted subjugation by armed minorities or by outside pressures." So was born the Truman Doctrine and, in December, 1947, an American military advisory group was set up in Athens to support the Greek Government.

The year 1948 was still touch and go. The Greek Army concentrated its main effort on trying to destroy the ELAS base areas in the mountains, thereby enabling the communists to extend their subversive and guerrilla activity in the unprotected populated areas inside the country.* ELAS fought well in defence of its bases and, in spite of suffering a reported 32,000 casualties, its strength at the end of the year was still about 23,000. Its raids into government-held populated areas followed the usual pattern and included the wholesale murder of government sympathisers. Nearly 25,000 recruits were kidnapped and over 23,000 children were abducted and taken behind the iron curtain. The use of terror by the KKE, publicised and condemned by the United Nations, was one of the worst features of the war and in the end contributed to the communist defeat.

The main causes of defeat were largely of the communists' own making. At the end of 1948 they committed the strategic blunder of changing the pattern of their military activity and going onto the offensive with the aim of directly defeating the Greek Army before its reorganisation and American aid had become fully effective. This was premature, and the reorganisation of units into conventional brigades, divisions and corps not only gave the Greek Army worthwhile targets but also reduced ELAS's contact with, and control of, the population. This was followed by a political error early in 1949 when Russia (through the Cominform) announced the intention of creating an independent Macedonian State. This rallied many nationalists and doubters to the government side. General Markos, himself as much a nationalist as a communist, who also favoured the continuation of small guerrilla

* Note the similar strategy adopted by the United States in Vietnam twenty years later with the same results. See also p. 59 for similar strategy by the Nationalists in China.

actions, was relieved of his command of ELAS and was succeeded by Zachariades. Russian policy towards Yugoslavia and Yugoslavia's defection from the bloc had already deprived ELAS of its most fruitful source of outside supply and support. The final closing of the Greek-Yugoslav frontier by Marshal Tito in July, 1949, also isolated the guerrilla forces operating on the Albanian border from those on the Bulgarian.

Nevertheless, the situation within Greece was still none too good. The government held the main towns but movement was still limited and convoys were always vulnerable to attack. Sabotage of communications and public utilities continued daily. In January, 1949, however, General Papagos, the hero of the Albanian campaign against Italy and a much respected forceful leader, was appointed Commander-in-Chief. With American help he reorganised the forces so that responsibility for static defence and the security of defended areas was given to the police and the national guard, thereby releasing the army for operations in a mobile role. He also reversed the previous plan of campaign. Using the minimum forces necessary to contain the rebels in their border mountain strongholds, he decided to concentrate the bulk of his forces first against the Peloponnese, secondly against central Greece, and finally against the main ELAS bases in the Vitsi and Grammos mountains. Just as important, he directed that the initial attack should be against the enemy's "infrastructure" in these areas in order to destroy his intelligence network and control over the population.

This proved most effective. All known communist sympathisers in the designated area were first rounded up so that the guerrilla forces, deprived of their intelligence, were quickly broken up by the government's mobile columns. By early spring, the Peloponnese had been cleared and by midsummer the same tactics had cleared central Greece. In August, having feinted first against the Grammos base area, the General then launched a concentrated attack against the Vitsi base area on the Albanian border. The guerrillas, about 7,500 strong, instead of withdrawing when faced with superior forces, decided to defend their base in the conventional tactics of positional war. This was a fatal error and by the middle of the month they were routed. A few remnants escaped through Albania to reinforce the Grammos base, to which General Papagos had so rapidly switched his forces that he was able to attack on 24 August. By the end of the month it was all over. The communists had lost not only their military forces but also any claim to popular support within Greece. They attempted to save face by announcing that they had ceased operations in order to preserve Greece from destruction.

In spite of their failure in Greece, the communists did however gain two long-term advantages. The first was the influence of the war on subsequent United States strategy and tactics in revolutionary war through a failure to analyse the reasons for the Greek Government success. Apart from the Russian political errors in causing the defection of Yugoslavia from the bloc and in promoting an independent State of Macedonia, the KKE itself made the basic military error of regrouping its forces at the end of 1948 in order to go over to a premature offensive instead of continuing to engage in protracted guerrilla warfare. This error was even more disastrous because it coincided with the loss of the Yugoslav supply base at the very moment when the regrouping of the forces into conventional units was bound to reduce the effectiveness of the insurgents' own supply base within Greece through loss of contact with the population. (A similar Vietcong loss of contact with the population from 1968 onwards in Vietnam was offset by the improved effectiveness of the Ho Chi Minh trail and supply routes through Cambodia.) Excessive use of terror tactics also contributed to this loss of contact. The military error was compounded when the ELAS forces, instead of withdrawing or dispersing in the summer of 1949, decided to hold their mountain bases using the conventional defensive tactics of positional war, thereby offering juicy targets for the fire-power of the well-equipped Greek Army.

On the government side there were also positive reasons for success stemming from the reorganisation of its forces at the beginning of 1949 and the appointment of General Papagos. The single control of operations and the mobility of the forces led to flexibility and gained the initiative for the government. The direction of the initial attack against the communist infrastructure within the country achieved the necessary dislocation of the enemy forces, and the direction of major operations against one area at a time in the right order achieved a concentration of force with the net result that, when it came down to dealing with the mountain bases in the final phase, the operations were both expeditious and decisive.

The spectacular success of these final battles tended to obscure the essential ingredients of the Greek victory, particularly in the military mind. It was to lead to American commanders in Vietnam later focusing their main attention on the enemy's base areas and relying for success on fire-power.

The second long-term advantage of the war was its subsequent influence on Greek politics and on the Greek Government's relations with its allies. The bitterness of such a brutal war was not to be eradicated in a generation, nor could the communist threat be forgotten. To those who have not experienced such a war or who do not have the imagination to realise its lasting psychological effect, it comes as a surprise that British seamen distributing communist leaflets in Greece should be arrested. Whatever the form of government, it would be surprising if they were not.

The Truman Doctrine of supporting free peoples resisting subjugation, prompted as it was by the Russian support for the communists in Greece, was to become a pillar of American foreign policy. It was followed by the Marshall Plan in Europe. Communist parties in those countries which were beyond the reach of the Soviet Army had been instructed to use the instrument of united front tactics and to join coalition governments wherever possible in the expectation that they would be able to exploit the political and economic confusion of post-war Europe which had been under German occupation. The Marshall Plan offered financial and economic assistance to all countries attempting to restore their damaged economies, even to those behind the iron curtain. Both Czechoslovakia and Poland wanted to accept, but the Soviet Government rejected the offer and put an end to the hopes of all the Eastern European countries which most needed it. As good orthodox communists the Russians first interpreted the Marshall Plan as American big business trying to open up new markets in Europe in order to avoid a depression in the United States, but the magnitude of the programme and its obvious altruism disproved this conclusion. It must, therefore, they argued, have an even more sinister interpretation—to recreate a Western Europe capable of maintaining large-scale military forces again. When coupled with other activities, such as Radio Free Europe, it looked to the Russians like a threat not just of containment but of their eventual liquidation. If, as they thought, the aim of the Plan was to re-arm Western Europe, the point might be reached where American satellites would be capable of taking on Russia's own satellites, thereby facing Russia with an agonising decision— whether to allow the frontiers of communism to be pushed back in central Europe or to intervene militarily in their defence and so risk American atomic weapons at a time when her own economic reconstruction was very limited and her own atomic armament non-existent (or over the next few years definitely inferior). While the success of the Marshall Plan put an end to any Russian hopes of a further advance in Europe, her fears were to prove unjustified. If anything, the Marshall Plan, because it encouraged the pursuit of an affluent society and an obsession with economic growth in all Western countries, led to a situation where their military and political influence in the post-war world steadily declined.

The Russian reaction was the creation of the Cominform* in 1947, explicitly dividing the world into two camps, and later the Comecon† in 1949, the latter being the Russian equivalent to the Plan. The focal point in the closing stage of the post-war struggle on this front was in Germany. The Allied integration of their three zones and the gradual build-up of a Federal Republic led to the Russian withdrawal from the Allied Control Commission and to the Berlin blockade as a means of bringing pressure to bear. Russia undoubtedly expected that there would be American and British reluctance to face her within her own domain, but she mistook the "terrain" in which the Allies were challenged. This was in the air where the Allies had the power. The blockade, defeated by the air-lift, had the effect of bringing the United States more firmly into Europe and led to the formation of the North Atlantic Treaty Organisation (NATO) which Russia answered with the Warsaw Pact. A sovereign State of West Germany emerged, to which the Russians replied by recognising the independence of East Germany. The Berlin wall eventually followed and the cold war in Europe reached a point of stalemate.

As the situation on the main front began to stabilise, Russian attention was switched to the eastern front where the cold war was warming up. Here it was to get very hot indeed with the communists winning the civil war in China, revolutionary wars being waged in several South East Asian countries, and the invasion of South Korea.

* Communist Information Bureau.
† Council for Mutual Economic Assistance.

4

China and South East Asia

THERE HAD been civil war between the communists
and the nationalists in China ever since the break
occurred between them in 1927. During the following ten years Mao Tse-tung, first in Hunan and Kiangsi
and later, after the "long march", in Shensi in north-
west China, developed his revolutionary war theory.
Originally Mao had thought that the revolution
could only be carried out by the urban proletariat in
the decisive role with support from mass uprisings in
the countryside, that the revolution would explode
spontaneously throughout the whole of China, and
that the struggle would be decided relatively
quickly. It took some years before he came to the
conclusions that the revolution would have to rely
basically on the peasantry, that rural base areas
would have to be established, from which the cities
could then be encircled but only after a prolonged
struggle, and that the revolutionary movement would
have to create an organised army. The basing of the
revolution on the peasants (Marx's "rustic idiots")
rather than on the proletariat was not entirely
approved as orthodox by the Soviet Union in the
Comintern period. However, the basis of the revolution was a secondary consideration to its success and
to Chinese subservience to Moscow, and Stalin,
according to the unimpeachable testimony of Chou
En-lai, gave considerable aid to the communist movement. The connection was, however, played down
and the first stories were put round to the effect that
the Chinese communists were not communists at all
but merely agrarian reformers. Japan had invaded
North China in 1931 and Russia did not want her
connection to provoke any risk of a deal between

Nationalist China and Japan which might destroy the revolution.

Moreover, because American support would be required for the defeat of Japan, Russia instructed the Chinese communists later in the 1930s to collaborate with the nationalists in the anti-Japanese war but herself, in accordance with her own policy of not being engaged on two fronts simultaneously, made a non-aggression pact with Japan in 1941. Just as the European communists had had to accept the Molotov-Ribbentrop Pact, so now the Chinese communists had to accept and rationalise this typical Russian manoeuvre.

In 1943 Russia agreed with her Western Allies to enter the war against Japan when the war in Europe was over and, in 1944, began to build up her military strength in the Far East. As in Europe, so here in Manchuria, Korea and North China there would obviously be opportunities for some choice pickings.

In 1945 the situation in China suggested to the Russians that Chiang Kai-shek with American support would be strong enough to stay in power but not to unite China. The communists would continue to control large areas of the north, thus limiting his power and American influence. Such a China could not possibly be a threat to Russia, and, by remaining friendly to the Nationalist Government, Russia should be able to obtain concessions along the border. (She had already seized and annexed Tannu Tuva in 1944.) The nationalists were, after all, the government of China and as such could formally agree to the transfer of Japanese-occupied territory to Russia, whereas the communists could not. It would therefore pay to remain friendly with the nationalists rather than to provoke a full-scale civil war immediately which Chiang might win or which, if he started to lose, might compel American intervention at a time when the United States still had forces in the area. Accordingly, on 14 August, 1945, Russia signed a treaty with the Nationalist Government under which she received concessions in Manchuria and North China and gave an undertaking not to recognise or help the communists. There was no outcry from the latter although the treaty seemed to indicate that, in the Russian national interest, they were expendable. Russian forces immediately occupied Manchuria and Korea down to the 38th Parallel, taking unnecessarily heavy casualties in order to make sure of a quick victory. A communist regime was installed in North Korea by the Soviet Army and the whole area was looted of its industrial equipment and machinery.

The United States had refused Russia any share in the occupation of Japan and it was to be expected that the United States would oppose Russian domination of China through the rising to power of Mao Tse-tung. It should be remembered that many Americans were still infatuated with the Nationalist China of Chiang Kai-shek. This infatuation stemmed from earlier American missionary and charitable work in China, from the public relations skill of Mme Chiang in the United States, and from a feeling that, as a new and struggling democracy complete with a "new life movement", China was the United States' cleanest ally. Americans felt a little guilty about being allied with imperialist Britain and communist Russia. Mr Harry Hopkins, the Presidential adviser, could even entertain the splendid fantasy that China and the United States together would spread democracy throughout the world. It was essential, therefore, for the Russians to camouflage the communist role and to revive the agrarian reform myth. Molotov so impressed Ambassador Hurley with this tale that the latter was led to assert that those supporting Mao in China were no more communists than Oklahoma Republicans! The Ambassador, in a subsequent interview with Stalin, then held forth to the effect that Mao was only interested in creating a free, democratic and united government in China, with which Stalin was happy to agree. In these circumstances the Russians had no difficulty in persuading the United States to take the initiative within China for reconciling Mao and Chiang in a coalition government. This put the responsibility on the United States to bring pressure to bear on the nationalists to be more democratic, more conciliatory and less corrupt and, at the same time, on the communists to work with the nationalists.*

The Americans were soon to become disenchanted with Chiang. Instant democracy was no more possible for him than it was for other leaders later who tended to rely for political power on the strength of United States' support rather than on local political compromise and manipulation. The Americans had hoped to achieve a united and democratic China, the

* Compare the similar ploy used in persuading Churchill to bring pressure on the Yugoslav monarchists to commit suicide by collaborating with Tito. Compare also the US pressure on South Vietnam in 1968-9 to come to terms with the NLF.

first only being obtainable if one side or the other won the civil war outright and the second always being illusory. A coalition government proved impossible and any question of dividing China was anathema to American politicians because it suggested spheres of influence. The net result was that the war had to be fought to a conclusion while the United States steadily reduced her bargaining position and also her influence on Chiang Kai-shek.

Meanwhile, in Manchuria, in spite of her treaty with the Nationalist Government, Russia allowed communist forces to enter outlying towns within the Soviet zone so that, when Soviet troops withdrew in May, 1946, the communists were able to occupy the whole of this important province. As a result of their own withdrawal, the Russians managed to persuade the Americans to withdraw their troops also from the rest of China, although they were there at the invitation of the Chinese Government. Stalin was able to make the point that Chiang would lose his influence if the Chinese people thought that his position depended on the presence of American troops. This solicitous concern for Chiang ensured that thereafter his aid was restricted to funds and equipment. Russia, however, was still very cautious. She did not foresee an early communist victory nor did she conceive that the United States would be prepared to let China go. The Chinese communists, on the other hand, with their belief in the great power of the Soviet Union as exemplified by the wartime victories, could not understand Russia's post-war internal weakness and her reluctance to confront the United States. This Soviet caution probably confirmed in some and planted in other Chinese communists their first suspicions of the Soviet Union. Mao correctly drew the conclusion that Soviet policy in relation to America was dictated by Russia's own national interests and fear of an American reaction rather than by absolute support for world revolutionary movements. There is no doubt that at this point Mao's assessment of great power politics and of the communist position within China itself was realistic. As soon as he had taken over the main centres in Manchuria he launched, contrary to Stalin's advice, a full-scale revolutionary war.

For this he was well prepared. His forces had been built up on a patriotic cause against Japan, and the American entry into the war had made it unnecessary for him to risk those forces in an offensive against the Japanese. They were retained (as in Greece) for the subsequent civil war while the United States defeated Japan. His occupation of Manchuria proved to be a snare for the nationalists. Just as in Greece the Greek Government initially deployed its main forces against the ELAS mountain bases, so now Chiang wasted his best troops in an attempt to reconquer Manchuria. Their defeat in 1947 proved almost decisive. The communist rural base areas throughout China were expanded and their armies, from a secure base on the Soviet frontier, were able to launch an all-out offensive (phase three of a revolutionary war). Within two years, by the end of 1949, this gave them the whole of China, so altering the balance of power in the world.

The communist victory was almost as much a shock to Russia as it was to the United States. In spite of the Chinese successes in 1947 and 1948, China had not been invited to become a founder member of the Cominform and Russia had been extremely reluctant to recognise even a provisional government in North China or to proclaim her support, still ostensibly out of fear that this might provoke a stronger American response in support of Chiang. Mao correctly and continually discounted this and it is certain that he has since interpreted the Russian caution as showing unwillingness to have a united China, even a communist one, on the Russian eastern frontier. Only in October, 1949, was Russia willing to recognise the Chinese People's Republic which was then proclaimed. Mao Tse-tung was invited to Moscow for two months' hard bargaining. In return for £300 million worth of credits over five years, Russia held on to the Manchurian railway and Port Arthur until 1952, and Peking recognised the independence of the Soviet-protected Mongolian People's Republic which, as Outer Mongolia, had been Chinese territory. Both Russia and the United States could rationalise the outcome on the basis that it would be years before China would be truly united or could develop into a military or industrial power. The United States was able to take refuge in further wishful thinking and the Secretary of State wrote: "Ultimately the profound civilisation and the democratic individualism of China will reassert themselves and she will throw off the foreign yoke." But it was not to be quite in the way that he hoped.

The immediate result for the United States was a period of recrimination, as expressed in the witch hunts carried out by Senator Joseph McCarthy against those responsible for the loss of China. From this period sprang the powerful China lobby supporting Chiang Kai-shek on Formosa and rigidly opposing any contact with the new China. The United States in subsequent policy was bound to adopt a hard line, particularly when the Korean war soon followed. Later involvement in Indo-China and South Vietnam and other commitments, such as the South East Asia Treaty Organisation (SEATO), were all designed to contain China and "Asian communism". While the policy itself was understandable, plausible (in line with that in Europe) and even desirable, the military aspect of the conflicts as they unfolded inclined the United States to view them as military problems and to seek therefore military solutions. Neither Greece nor China, as revolutionary wars, had any influence on the American conventional military approach to war.

In the rest of Asia, especially in South East Asia, the Soviet approach in the immediate post-war years was very similar to that in those countries of Europe which had been beyond the reach of the Soviet Army. Communist parties were encouraged to adopt united front tactics, to enter coalitions or to collaborate, even with colonial governments, so that party influence, greatly enhanced by the war particularly where it had led resistance movements, could be extended through continued penetration of trade unions, student unions and other political associations. This was the case in India, Indonesia, Malaya, the Philippines, Burma and Japan. This approach also partly accounted for Ho Chi Minh's initial attempt in Indo-China to reach a political agreement with the French Government of which the French Communist Party was then a member. After the founding of the Cominform in September, 1947, by which time the Russian position in the satellites on her southern front was reasonably secure, the policy changed to a more violent approach as the cold war developed.

The general situation at the beginning of 1948 dictated the next Russian moves. The United States had now become involved in the war in Greece; the coup was taking place in Czechoslovakia; the quarrel with Yugoslavia was reaching its climax; tension was rising on the German question with the Berlin blockade about to begin; and in China Mao Tse-tung, having driven Chiang out of Manchuria, was starting his main offensive. From the Soviet point of view her two more important fronts were secure and certainly not threatened. In each area of conflict the Russians were able to pursue an activist forward policy to extend communist control further beyond their frontiers. If successful this policy would represent a great victory but, if it failed, no great harm would necessarily be done to the Soviet base. It was in essence a might-not-win but could-not-lose policy. This therefore seemed the ideal moment, partly as a diversion, to spread the scope of the conflict by making use of communist parties in other territories as a means of advancing both aims of her foreign policy.

In February, 1948, a communist conference, ostensibly of "Democratic Youth", was held in Calcutta attended by representatives of communist parties from all over the world, including all the South East Asian territories. A thesis was accepted that the correct form of struggle at this stage was "armed struggle". Within a few weeks armed insurgency had broken out in Indonesia, Burma, Malaya and the Philippines. The revolutionary war in Indo-China was already in phase two. There is now little doubt that instructions for insurgency were issued at the conference by the central party in Moscow. The circumstantial evidence to this effect is overwhelming, not least in the fact that some members of the communist parties concerned considered an uprising premature but were overruled, and the coincidence of the timing is itself almost conclusive. At this period all communist parties, including the Chinese, were subservient to Moscow and, in any case, the Chinese communists were in full agreement with such a change of tactics. Mao took the line that militant action in Asia would not provoke such an imperialist reaction as to be a threat to the Soviet Union. His argument was that outbreaks of insurgency would instead increase the contradictions in the imperialist camp. Palme Dutt of the British Communist Party summed up the favourable situation when he wrote: "The whole region of South East Asia is today the central arena of the struggle for national liberation against imperialism. The approaching victory of democratic China heralds a new era in Asia." So began the first great wave of revolutionary wars in South East Asia coinciding with the critical year of those in Greece and China.

By the end of 1949 the British were fully engaged with the Emergency in Malaya; the Americans, in support of the newly independent Philippines Government, with the Hukbalahap insurgency; and the French with the Vietminh war in Indo-China, where, the French Communist Party having withdrawn its collaboration with the French Government after the 1948 decision, there was no further attempt made at a political settlement. Only in Indonesia did the uprising fail. Here it had in reality been no more than an attempted coup which was crushed at once in West Java by the best division in the Indonesian National Army. This failure, together with that in Greece, was more than offset by the success of Mao in China. However, with the failure of the Berlin blockade the situation in Europe stabilised although the main issue of the future of Germany was unresolved. The Far East remained the active area and a further opportunity for expansion soon presented itself in Korea.

All American proposals, made in accordance with wartime agreements, for elections to be held leading to the reunification of North and South Korea were rejected by the Russians who had already turned their zone into a satellite communist State. When a general election was finally held in the South under United Nations auspices, leading to the election of Syngman Rhee as first head of the South Korean Government, the Russians in the North established a People's Democracy on the East European model. Soviet citizens remained in official positions and a North Korean Army was created on Soviet lines. There was no question during this period of the North Korean Government being in a position to take any independent action on its own account.

What followed was entirely a Soviet decision. On 12 January, 1950, Mr Dean Acheson, the American Secretary of State, having been advised by the Chiefs of Staff that America had little strategic interest in Korea, stated that South Korea would have to depend for its defence on its own efforts and rely on its position as a member of the United Nations. He followed this up later, in May, 1950, by suggesting that South Korea was militarily untenable. The Russian reaction to the first statement was to increase the North Korean Army of four divisions and a few border brigades to six divisions while a further seven divisions were formed. Soon after the second statement, on 25 June, 1950, the first six divisions and three border brigades crossed the frontier on the 38th Parallel and invaded South Korea.

Quite apart from Dean Acheson's statement, the Russians had no reason to expect that this attack would provoke any United States reaction. After all, the United States had let the whole of China (except Formosa) fall into communist hands and there seemed no reason why she should now intervene to save a small peninsula on the Asian mainland that was of no strategic interest to her. Nor was the Security Council, from which Russia had temporarily withdrawn, expected to act. Once again, as before in Greece, the American response proved unpredictable and unreliable for the Russians. President Truman took immediate steps through the United Nations to meet the threat. A United Nations force under the command of General MacArthur repulsed the invasion and, through landings at Inchon, had by September regained the 38th Parallel. The North Korean Army was routed and the advance continued into North Korea, reaching almost to the Yalu River on the border with China.

There was now every prospect that North Korea would be lost and that it would not be possible to restore peace even on the basis of the status quo. The Russian attempt to use a satellite army as an instrument of policy had completely failed. Intervention would be necessary but Russia herself could not risk turning a limited war into a global war at a time when only the United States had the bomb. The task therefore fell upon the Chinese. There is some doubt as to whether the Chinese communists were even consulted about the invasion of South Korea, but now they did not hesitate to go to the rescue of the North. The Chinese 4th Field Army was already in Manchuria and the move of her 3rd Field Army northwards from Central China showed that she was prepared to do more than just defend her own frontiers. The Chinese offensive across the Yalu River recovered North Korea down to the 38th Parallel but subsequent offensives failed to achieve any further breakthrough to the south. It was enough and the Russians put out the first peace feelers in June, 1951. This, however, did not end the fighting and the peace talks at Panmunjom went on for two years with the United States suffering about 80,000 casualties. Delaying tactics at the conference table were designed to wear out the Allies and thereby gain further concessions. After the death of Stalin in March, 1953, the communist negotiators became more conciliatory, particularly with regard to the exchange of prisoners, and in July an armistice was signed.

Apart from showing that the Russians were prepared to take anything that seemed to be offered, the Korean war's chief lesson was that in the event of failure they would not be prepared to cut their losses to the extent of deserting a communist State already in being. While they might be prepared to give up the purpose of any particular adventure, their obligation, because of the example it might set, to maintain an existing communist government in power and the integrity of its territory was absolute.

Meanwhile in South East Asia revolutionary war was not proving an unqualified success. The communists were losing in both Malaya and the Philippines and were making no headway in Burma. Only in Indo-China was success on the way, partly because the Chinese since 1950 had been in a position to give material support to the Vietminh against the French.

In Malaya, whereas the Malayan Communist Party had succeeded in gaining control of the resistance movement during the Japanese occupation, it failed subsequently as a legal political party in post-war Malaya to secure the support of the bulk of the population in a movement designed to achieve independence under the leadership of the communist party. The issue here was less independence, because that had been explicitly promised by the British, than the succession to power, i.e. who would take over when the British left. The Malay nationalist movement represented by the United Malay National Organisation (UMNO), the (mainly Indian) trade unions and the more conservative Chinese all came out on the side of the government. In this respect, therefore, the party failed to hold "space" and represented only a small minority in the country. Nevertheless the threat was severe and, by 1951, the government's resources were stretched to the utmost. The subsequent success of the government can be attributed to the basic plan of General Sir Harold

Briggs, which directed the attack on the enemy's infrastructure within the population and which re-settled about 500,000 of the scattered rural Chinese population from the guerrilla units; to Field-Marshal control from the communist party and isolating the population from the guerrilla units; to Field-Marshal Sir Gerald Templer for his dynamic drive in imple-menting this plan until the remaining guerrilla units were driven back into their jungle bases where they could be systematically eliminated; to Sir Henry Gurney, the High Commissioner from 1948 to 1951, when he was killed in a communist ambush, for placing the initial emphasis on maintaining a strong administrative structure and the rule of law; and to Tunku Abdul Rahman, the first Prime Minister of independent Malaya, and other local leaders for sup-porting these measures and for showing the deter-mination to continue the war after 1955 through a long mopping-up period of five years until complete victory had been achieved. Special features of the war were the creation of a single highly efficient in-telligence organisation within the police force, the arming of villagers, both Malay and Chinese, to de-fend their own villages and a well-publicised reward system. In effect the general strategy of the war was not unlike that in the final stages of the Greek cam-paign, although the time taken was very much longer because the guerrilla units dispersed and continued guerrilla warfare instead of standing and fighting.

Another special feature of the Malayan campaign was the emphasis placed on "winning the hearts and minds of the people", which was to have considerable influence on the conduct of subsequent counter-insurgencies. In this respect it is worth bearing in mind Mao's famous statement that "political power grows out of a barrel of a gun" and the remark made by the Russian General Skobelev, who conquered Turkestan and captured Tashkent in 1877, that "in Asia he is master who seizes the people pitilessly by the throat". There is no doubt that, in winning the hearts and minds, the government must show by its performance, first, that it intends to and can win and, secondly, that it can protect the population. The benefits then follow. One essential point is that these economic, social and other benefits should be conferred through the administrative machine of the country thereby inculcating a sense of permanence and normality to the situation in government-held areas. If the first two points are not made and benefits are conferred, no matter how lavishly, through outside agencies, the whole effort will be wasted. Hearts and minds cannot be won by bribery alone.

In the Philippines, where the communist party had been formed in 1930 and admitted to the Comintern in 1932, the Hukbalahap (originally the People's Army against Japan) was founded by the party under Luis Taruc in 1942. The Huks, who were in conflict with other guerrilla groups throughout the Japanese occupation, numbered about 15,000 on the island of Luzon and caused considerable disruption to Japanese supplies north of Manila. Little recognition was given to their efforts after the re-occupation and Taruc himself was arrested but later released. It was this group under the communist party with a strength of about 20,000 men which was re-activated in 1948. After early successes during which they roamed freely over most of Luzon with their politbureau actually operating from within Manila itself, they were defeated by the imaginative strategy of the Minister of Defence and later President, Raymond Magsaysay, with American support. The armed forces were reorganised to give greater mobility, land was offered to the Huks on other islands and a reward system was introduced. By 1954 the movement was broken and Taruc himself surrendered. Minor activity continued for some years until the army was eventually relieved of its internal security duties in 1958, after the death of Magsaysay in an air crash. Here again the Huks were unrepresentative of the bulk of the population and, when the people were rallied by Magsaysay working in accordance with the constitution, communism was defeated by nationalism.

In Burma the communist party was itself split into the Red and White Flags, while the Burmese Government had also to contend with dissident ethnic minorities in its border hill provinces such as the Kerens, Kachins, Chins and Shans. A low-scale insurgency combined with endemic banditry continues to this day, complicated by the variety of the many dissidents and by Chinese meddling both along the frontier and in support of the White Flags. Whereas the other communist parties in South East Asia were able to claim, at least ostensibly, that they were fighting for independence, socialism and neutrality, which appeared in all their manifestos, the Communist Party of Burma, when it broke with the government in 1948 and launched its insurrection after the Calcutta conference, could not advance such a cause because the government of Burma was itself indisputably independent, socialist and neutral. The party was fighting solely to seize power, as indeed were all the others.

In Indo-China the situation was very different and had been so from the beginning in 1945. The Indo-China Communist Party under Ho Chi Minh had led what little local resistance there was to the Japanese occupation and, more important, by establishing the nationalist front known as the Vietminh, had laid the best claim to leadership of the nationalist cause for independence from the French. Moreover, in the chaotic conditions which prevailed in 1945 the communist party was able to eliminate the leaders of other rival nationalist movements, to compel the abdication of the Emperor Bao Dai, who had already denounced the French treaties of protection, and to proclaim a republic, using the terminology of the American declaration of independence. Russia at this early stage, because of its relations with the post-war French Government, of which the communist party was a member, offered neither recognition nor aid. When all attempts up to 1948 had failed to achieve a negotiated solution between Ho Chi Minh and the French Government, on the ground that the latter's offers were always too little and too late, a full-scale revolutionary war was launched throughout Indo-China.

The decisive actions of the war were fought mainly in the Red River Delta area of Tonkin and in the surrounding mountain jungles up to the Chinese frontier, but the Vietminh threat to the French was spread throughout the whole of Indo-China, including Laos and Cambodia. Several provinces in Vietnam were never, or only temporarily, re-occupied by the French. By the end of 1950 the French were driven out of, or had evacuated, all the border towns on the Chinese frontier, suffering considerable losses in the process. The whole of the Viet Bac, surrounding the Red River Delta to the north and west, was in Vietminh hands. The Vietnamese general, Vo Nguyen Giap, then made his only strategic mistake of the war by attempting to engage the French, now commanded by Marshal de Lattre de Tassigny, in open warfare in the Red River Delta itself. He was bloodily repulsed and retreated to the continuation of guerrilla warfare, as required in phase two of a revolutionary war. With increasing supplies now coming from China the Vietminh were able to maintain a high scale of activity and, by the end of 1953, the equivalent of two Vietminh divisions were operating inside the French controlled zone based on Hanoi and the port of Haiphong. The road between these two vital towns could be kept open only for a few hours every afternoon. It took the French most of the morning to clear the mines which had been laid overnight. In a last attempt to force the Vietminh to fight a conventional battle the French then made their great strategic blunder of establishing a heavily garrisoned post in the obscure town and valley of Dien Bien Phu beyond the range of effective air support.

Meanwhile, on the political front, in a vain endeavour to rally the anti-communist nationalists to their cause, the French had established a Vietnamese government under the ex-Emperor Bao Dai within the French Union. Never were they prepared to grant full independence and this political failure proved disastrous to their cause. The French proposal was not a credible alternative. Although French troops fought well, the basic cause of defeat can be attributed to the vacillation and ineptitude of the French Government —or rather French Governments (there were fifteen between 1945 and 1954).

In spite of the Vietminh success, there was still no certainty early in 1954 that the French would be quickly or eventually defeated. Even if they lost the impending battle of Dien Bien Phu, there was still a grave risk that the United States, extremely angry after Korea and the stalling of negotiations at Panmunjom, might do more than help the French with equipment and financial support, as they had been doing since the Korean war in 1950, and become directly involved in the war. It was partly the reluctance of the British Government to support the intervention of the American Air Force at Dien Bien Phu which kept the United States out. It seemed, therefore, to the new leaders of Russia after Stalin's death that the time had come for disengagement, consolidation and a re-appraisal of policy.

5

From Co-existence to the Sino-Soviet Dispute

A GOOD case can be made for the argument that the first wave of revolutionary wars in South East Asia supported by Russia in 1948 were premature. They alerted nationalist movements in most territories to the communist threat and, when combined with Korea, united the West to resist communist expansion. The ineptitude of Russian propaganda during this period with its abusive attacks on the Allied war effort, notably on the Arctic convoys and the bombing of Germany as being of little account, all of which were designed to bolster the claim that Russia had won the war single-handed, did not help the communist cause. The promotion of the World Peace Council, because the propaganda attached to it was so clearly out of line with Soviet action, was too hypocritical and transparent to make any impression on Western public opinion except for confirmed fellow-travellers. The two communist successes in China and Indo-China were basically Chinese and Vietminh victories for which Russia could take only incidental credit. Nevertheless, the other pawns in South East Asia were not entirely sacrificed and underground communist parties, though greatly weakened, remained in being ready to rise again when the opportunity offered.

The death of Stalin and the East German uprising in 1953, put down by Russian tanks, led to a situation where the new leaders of Russia were prepared to seek a detente in Europe and a settlement in Korea and Indo-China. The Berlin Conference at the beginning of 1954 failed, however, to secure any settlement in Europe on the German question or the Austrian Peace

Treaty, and the attention of all governments concerned was switched to the Far East where the war in Indo-China was reaching a climax at Dien Bien Phu. There is no doubt that the Russians and the Chinese (who at this time were still aligned with Russia) brought pressure on the Vietminh to reach a settlement which compelled General Giap, as the Geneva conference opened, to seek a quick military victory at an enormous cost in lives in order to break the French will to continue fighting and to obtain the best possible terms. Some now claim that the Vietminh were disappointed at the result which required them to evacuate Laos and Cambodia, where independent States were established, and to agree to the partition of Vietnam at the 17th Parallel. But they themselves first put forward the idea of partition and it seems likely that both they and the Malenkov government were influenced by the practical certainty of being able to establish a new communist State in North Vietnam through accepting an immediate settlement and thereby eliminating the risk of direct American intervention.

Malenkov was in a way following in Stalin's footsteps by using the communist tactic of recognising a revolutionary movement as a government, thereby turning an area in which a guerrilla army was operating into a communist State. (The same tactic was to be employed again by Brezhnev in 1969 when the National Liberation Front in South Vietnam was recognised as a provisional government.) Even if the whole of Vietnam could not be secured, an extensive gain of territory in the North could be consolidated and used as a base for a further advance later. France paid the Russian price for the compromise settlement by refusing to ratify the agreement on a European Defence Community. This, however, did not prevent West Germany becoming a member of NATO as a sovereign State. The subsequent Russian refusal to consider the reunification of Germany on the basis of free all-German elections, under which West Germany would have out-voted East Germany, is interesting in the light of her subsequent support for a similar election in Vietnam in 1956 as proposed under the Geneva Agreements. The answer was that, if she did not like it in Germany,* she could not have it in Vietnam.

The major influence inclining the Russians to a policy of co-existence was a re-assessment of nationalism in the newly independent territories of Asia. The failure of the revolutionary wars and of the communist parties in India and elsewhere prompted Russia to adopt the well-known tactic—if you cannot lick it, join it. Russia had at first been hostile to all the new nationalist governments and treated them as the tools and puppets of imperialism. For example, in 1949 Gandhi was regarded as a traitor to the national liberation movement but, by 1955, Russian history had been re-written to make him a hero. Similarly, in Burma, U Nu had been castigated for suppressing the national liberation movement but, in 1954 and 1955, he was visiting Peking and Moscow (where a trade agreement was signed to obtain Burmese rice urgently needed to relieve starvation in the new communist State of North Vietnam). A five-year trade

* Or, for that matter, in Korea.

agreement had already been signed with the Indian
Government in 1953 and Nehru was given a tumul-
tuous welcome in Moscow on his State visit in 1955.
Khrushchev paid his famous Asian visit to India,
Burma and Indonesia in 1955 and a massive Russian
Embassy was established in Bangkok. This was the
year of the Bandung Conference where the Chinese
Premier, Mr Chou En-lai, made such a great impression and the five principles of co-existence were
reaffirmed by India and accepted. These included
mutual respect for territorial integrity, non-aggression, and non-interference in the internal affairs of
another State for any reason. This was the era for
China of "let a hundred flowers bloom, let a hundred
schools of thought contend", which was more cynically interpreted as "only by letting the weeds show
themselves can they be uprooted". It was this latter
interpretation which was about to occupy Russia on
her southern and most important front.

After the Russian split with Yugoslavia drastic
purges had been carried out in the satellite States and
continued even after Stalin's death. In 1956, however,
came the attack on Stalinism delivered in a speech by
Khrushchev at the 20th Party Congress. The accusations made against Stalin were shattering to communist parties throughout the world and their
immediate effect was to spark off the Poznan riots in
Poland, which brought Russian leaders, including
Marshal Bulganin, post-haste to Warsaw to announce
that the riots were entirely provoked by enemy
agents seeking to restore capitalism. However, the
Polish Communist Party itself retained control of
the situation by making concessions to the workers

and by agreeing to a degree of liberalisation which included the re-admission of Mr Gomulka to the party. The party succeeded in carrying the population with it, which made it unnecessary for Russia to intervene with force. The situation in Hungary was very different. Here the move for a more liberal and democratic approach took place outside the party and was opposed by the party leaders who failed to stem the revolt. Russian intervention was compelled by Nagy's announcement of Hungary's neutrality and withdrawal from the Warsaw Pact. Unlike Poland, this was secession and Soviet troops, after an initial defeat in Budapest, re-occupied the whole country in overwhelming force.

Although the Hungarian uprising and the manner in which it was put down made a profound impression in the West, it had a lesser effect on Asian and Middle Eastern countries than the Suez campaign which coincided with it. In accordance with her change of strategy Russia had already identified herself with Arab nationalism and, as a means of gaining influence, was already purchasing surplus raw materials, especially Egyptian cotton and rice, and selling arms to the area. By 1956 over one-third of Egypt's external trade was with the communist bloc and the Russian trade gap of £10m was balanced by the sale of Soviet arms (carefully routed through Czechoslovakia to avoid too direct a commitment of Russian military prestige). While Russia supported Egypt's nationalisation of the Suez Canal in July, 1956, and presented the crisis as one between imperialism and national liberation, she wanted to be in on any settlement which might be reached because she needed the Canal to develop her new strategy* and because she could not risk the future hostility of an Egyptian government which, though nationalist, was still anti-communist.

The outbreak of war between Egypt and Israel and the intervention of Britain and France presented Russia with an awkward problem. She hurriedly evacuated her Ilyushin bombers and technicians from Egypt through the Sudan. When her implied threat to use nuclear weapons was countered by an American warning, she then proposed, as a means of getting Russian troops into the Middle East, joint American and Russian intervention, which was rejected by the United States. A belated threat to send volunteers was obviously never meant to be carried out. Nevertheless, Suez had its advantages for Russia by heralding the eclipse of British and French influence in the Middle East and by creating a rift between the United States and her Western Allies. It also confirmed Russia's role as the supporter of Arab nationalism. The military defeat of Egypt, however, by the Israelis and the ignominious withdrawal of Russian aircraft and technicians provided one hard lesson, that trade and aid would be ineffective until there was greater Soviet military penetration of the area to lend weight to any Russian threat of intervention and to make it more plausible as a political and diplomatic weapon.

During the period of co-existence in the post-Stalin years, Russia's target areas were India, Burma, the Middle East, Indonesia and Africa through the

* By 1969, with the Canal already closed for two years, Russia's need for it was becoming more apparent.

tactics of political and economic penetration and the
avoidance of uncontrolled violence, because excessive
local unrest only hindered the economic offensive of
subversion through trade. It should be noted here
that in any conflict Russia has always tended to support the side with the greatest numbers—China
against Japan, the Arabs against Israel, India against
Pakistan, the Indonesians in South East Asia and,
later, Nigeria against Biafra. In her approach to the
Third World Russia was developing a strategy where
local instability had to be kept manageable and where
conflicts and revolutionary wars could only be promoted provided that they could be curbed and controlled within the limits required to maintain a
minimum degree of world order.

It had been Stalin's final directive on foreign
policy that Russia should attempt to split the United
States from her allies, with particular reference to
France, Britain and Japan. It was the United States
which was now singled out as the target for a concerted propaganda attack. Russia had always represented the American post-war presence in Europe as a
form of invasion. It was a penetration of the European-Asian land mass, where Russia regarded herself
as the leading power, by the leading power of the
American land mass. NATO came constantly under
attack and Russia's disarmament proposals at this
time were designed to reduce nuclear armaments,
where she had inferiority, without reducing conventional armaments, where she had superiority. Pressure
was again brought to bear on Berlin through Khrushchev's threat to hand over all Russian rights to East
Germany and to recognise it. This was firmly opposed

by a united West and Khrushchev's time limit on the ultimatum was extended and then quietly dropped. After his visit to the United States in 1959 he was prepared to seek a closer understanding, but the American U2 flights over Russia compelled him to take a tougher line in order to maintain his position with the party, which was still critical of any detente with the enemy. It was Khrushchev's view that an apparent detente in the vital area of Europe would give Russia a better opportunity for steadily undermining the influence of the West in the Third World. If a detente was not possible, then it had to be deadlock and this followed with the building of the Berlin wall.

If Russia's aims of weakening the Western Alliance, of conducting a political and economic offensive in the Third World and of improving her military mobility through a naval and air transport build-up were to be successful, then she also had to secure her eastern flank and retain a reliable and obedient China as its bastion. In the aftermath of the Korean and Indo-China wars the Chinese, in spite of increased military expenditure, bringing it to 22 per cent of the budget, were conciliatory in accordance with the Bandung principles of co-existence and accepted the Soviet line. China was still dependent on Russia for arms and aid which had to be paid for in her own exports, although this led in turn to food shortages and a lack of consumer goods. While China remained dependent on Soviet economic aid, she supported Soviet policy, even on Hungary, so that Russia's eastern flank was stabilised. China was also influenced by Soviet military strength, the development of

ICBM's and the launching of the first Sputnik. While Russia fully supported China in her claims to the off-shore islands of Quemoy and Matsu (and in her more intensive bombardment of them during 1958), to Formosa and to membership of the United Nations and a seat on the Security Council, she did not, however, approve the extension of Chinese control into the Himalays nor China's domestic policy of "the great leap forward" and the development of the communes as a means of accelerating the advance of communism. The Chinese occupation of Tibet in 1959, which led to the flight of the Dalai Lama, hastened the clash between China and India. China's frontier claims were not supported by Russia and a further rift occurred as a result of Khrushchev's visit to the United States, regarded by China since the Korean war as the implacable enemy. This led on to arguments over the inevitability of war which is at the root of the ideological clash between Russia and China. Lenin and Stalin had looked on war between communism and capitalism as inevitable and even desirable as a short cut to communism. But this view now had to be modified in the light of the nuclear reality of an "assured destruction capability", which ruled out any question of a pre-emptive strike. Russia had to guard against the danger of miscalculation and the risk of being dragged over the brink by China. She therefore maintained that nuclear war would not hasten the victory of communism, while China still claimed that "Socialism, far from being destroyed, would be achieved all the more quickly in the event of war." In this respect China was not necessarily advocating directly aggressive policies but she did feel that Soviet military strength allowed much greater risks to be taken. China also began to question Russia's aid to the Third World as a means of weaning countries like India and Egypt from the West, since it did not bring them within the communist bloc. To China such aid was worthless and ought instead to be given either to communist powers or to assist revolutionary movements under the leadership of the communist party.

The first great myth that the Chinese communists were no more than agrarian reformers had already been proved false. Now the second great myth that China was no more than a willing obedient satellite of Russia was about to be exploded—but not to the West's advantage as earlier American statesmen had hoped. To understand this it is necessary to take a brief look at China's past history and view of the world.

From time immemorial China has always regarded herself as the centre of the world, as her name of the Central Kingdom (Chunk Kuo) implies. In the fertile plains along her great rivers she had been able to develop her own civilisation and language almost undisturbed. She experienced no dark ages and there was no break in her literature nor the record of her history. All her people were Chinese by race and nationality and there were no separate nations as in Europe, only the distinction between the civilised Chinese and the barbarians beyond her frontiers. There was always a sense of unity even if it was not always expressed in an effective political form. This unity was assured both by the numerical strength of the Chinese population and by the natural boundaries of deserts, mountains, jungle and sea. Within these boundaries China felt secure and all alien influences could be rejected except those which contained no political threat, such as the Buddhist religion. At worst any would-be conqueror could be absorbed. Almost exactly one thousand years ago, under the T'ang dynasty, China was richer and better developed than any other area in the world, and also better governed by a well-educated, trained and publicly recruited civil service which helped to maintain continuing stability throughout the country in spite of subsequent dynastic changes. Outside contact with traders and missionaries (both Arab and Christian) made little impression until the armed traders of the West appeared in the nineteenth century.

The greater power of the West and growing disintegration within China itself, resulting in the frequent humiliation of the government of China, led to a conflict between conservatism and modernisation, between those who wanted to cling to the old traditions as a means of driving out the foreigner and the reformers who saw the need for modern weapons, even if they did not immediately see the need for other forms of industrial and political development which went with them. The reforming message was that salvation lay in western learning and political theory but the recipe failed in China, although it succeeded in Japan. The Empire fell into the hands of military adventurers and civil war followed. Of all the previous institutions only the schools and universities remained and, after World War I and the Russian Revolution, the student youth was already attracted by the teaching of the left before a communist party was formed. During the 1920s and 1930s both nationalists and communists were aiming to restore China to her rightful place. When in 1949 the Mandate of Heaven passed to Mao Tse-tung, the old Empire was restored in a new form.

In all her past history China had never had to deal with allies on an equal footing because her many neighbours had been either tributaries or enemies. Foreign policy was, therefore, seldom envisaged in terms of alliances or of a balance of power but rather as a matter of maintaining China's rightful sphere of influence. Her association with the allies in World War I only resulted in Tsing Tao being transferred from Germany to Japan. This served to confirm that a strong China needed no allies and that a weak China would obtain no benefit from them. China had no friends, therefore, when Japan attacked in 1931 and the alliances, subsequently formed in World War II after Pearl Harbor, were caused by events and not by any conscious line of foreign policy on the part of China. They did not save the Nationalist Government, which had made them, after the war. The alliance of the Chinese People's Republic with Russia was dictated by their temporary ideological affiliation rather than by mutual national interests and it took a two-month visit to Moscow by Mao Tse-tung himself to make it. It gave the Chinese only arms and equipment in return for economic dependence on Russia and political support for her claims to Formosa, the off-shore islands and the Chinese seat on the Security Council, but no direct assistance for her territorial defence or support for her traditional claims beyond her existing borders (including that with Russia). Ideological ties were not enough and the honeymoon was short-lived.

Traditionally China has been isolationist and memories of Tsarist imperialism and the half-heartedness of Soviet support in the post-war years soon undermined the harmony. Russian support for Outer Mongolia, India and Indonesia (particularly in view of Sukarno's policy towards the overseas Chinese population) put Russia in a position where she was trespassing on China's preserves against Chinese influence and interest. This rivalry was later to intensify both in Vietnam and on their common borders. Even on the ideological front there was a strong element of the Chinese traditional concept of her own position in the world. When she claimed that her revolution was the pattern for all under-developed territories in the Third World and that she alone correctly interpreted the Marxist-Leninist doctrine, thereby competing with Russia for the leadership of the communist world, it was no more than a re-statement of her traditional view that China was the centre of the civilised world and the model for all to copy. By treating Marx almost as a Chinese sage China was giving communism an oriental base so that the new emperor and his thoughts were again the fount of all wisdom.

Russia could then be denounced for being bourgeois and revisionist, frightened of nuclear war and therefore ready to betray the revolution in favour of co-existence, with which China had only briefly flirted, thereby prolonging the existence of capitalist society. The paper tigers of imperialism held no fear for China and she was therefore prepared to promote revolution-

ary war in all areas and to risk, though not directly
to provoke, a wider war. According to Mao's analysis,
wars are won by men and not by machines and China
had the former in abundance. By combining purity of
doctrine with material strength, Mao had succeeded in
bringing Confucius up to date. In practice, however,
China has been extremely cautious. She will always
proclaim the doctrine loud and clear but, if it cannot
be followed in practice, that must never be admitted.
This is the sort of fiction with which China has always been able to live. Her only fear in her in-
creasingly independent and isolated position was
that Russia might do a deal with the United States
at her expense. However, by adopting a hard and
intransigent line on revolutionary wars and advancing
her own claim to their leadership, she has faced the
Russians with the dilemma either of going part of the
way with her or of forfeiting their own claim to world
communist leadership, which itself would result in a
complete split and seriously weaken Russia's position
on her two main fronts. At the same time, by inten-
sifying her ideological quarrel with the United States
to the point of hatred, she has succeeded in transfer-
ring it to the nationalist plane over her claims to the
off-shore islands and Formosa and to South East Asia
as her sphere of influence, thereby justifying her stand
domestically and at the same time keeping the United
States and Russia apart in this area in rival positions.
In this way China has achieved a position where the
West can derive little benefit from the split and where
Russia on any issue with the West must reluctantly,
and in the last resort certainly, support her.

In relation to revolutionary war itself the split has

developed both on method and on direction. Russia, although in theory supporting revolutionary war and in practice being prepared to use it as an instrument of expansion at a suitable opportunity, is quite content, in pursuing her strategy of subversion through trade and aid while extending her military penetration through increased mobility, to allow non-communists to carry out the first stage of a revolution (as did Kerensky in Russia) in the expectation that the communist party will eventually succeed to power. (The Sudan is providing a good example.) This later take-over can be encouraged, if not actively promoted, by Russian political and economic support for an existing non-communist but revolutionary government leading to a situation where it becomes dependent and therefore vulnerable to further pressure. This approach is slow, steady and cautious in that it minimises the risk, because the process of erosion is so gradual, of any *volte face* on the part of the target and of any confrontation with the United States. Russia can work on the principle that one revolutionary and unstable government can succeed another, provided that none is pro-Western, because, when the turn of the communist party comes, it only has to win once.

The Chinese, on the other hand, insist that the communist party must be in the vanguard of the revolution from the start and in full control throughout, which automatically creates a risk that the threatened government will seek outside support leading to Western and in particular United States involvement. Under the Russian method the local communist party can maintain relations with an existing government and even act, on a united front pattern, in a constitutional manner, whereas Mao Tse-tung maintains that the party must be uncompromisingly hostile to an existing non-communist government and seek its overthrow.

The basic document setting forth the Chinese view is the long speech by Marshal Lin Piao made in September, 1965, on "Long Live the Victory of People's War", which repeated the Chinese line laid down since 1949 and developed it further. After referring to the lessons of the war against Japan and the party's victory in China, he turned to the future international significance of Mao's theory of revolutionary war and quoted Mao's point that:

> The seizure of power by armed force, the settlement of the issue by war, is the central task and the highest form of revolution. This Marxist-Leninist principle of revolution holds good universally, for China and for all other countries.

Drawing on the parallel of the civil war in China, where the revolution was based on the countryside and where the countryside was used to encircle the cities, he then stated:

> Taking the entire globe, if North America and Western Europe can be called the "cities of the world", then Asia, Africa and Latin America constitute "the rural areas of the world". . . . In a sense the contemporary world revolution also presents a picture of the encirclement of cities by the rural areas. In the final analysis the whole cause of world revolution hinges on the revolutionary

struggles of the Asian, African and Latin-American peoples who make up the overwhelming majority of the world's population. The socialist countries should regard it as their internationalistic duty to support the people's revolutionary struggles in Asia, Africa and Latin America.

He re-emphasised that the revolution could only be led by the proletariat and a genuinely revolutionary party armed with Marxism-Leninism and by no other class or party. For China the enemy is United States imperialism which can only be defeated by revolutionary war. Finally he castigated the Khrushchev revisionists as the betrayers of revolutionary war because "they have no faith in the masses and are afraid of United States imperialism, of war and of revolution". The Khrushchev line of peaceful co-existence, peaceful transition and peaceful competition is derided as rubbish. Firm Chinese support and active aid is promised to those waging revolutionary wars.

That is the doctrine, on which Chinese policy and strategy is based, in all its purity but, if in practice it cannot always be exactly followed, that will never be admitted. The doctrine will still be loudly proclaimed.

6

Africa and Latin America

THE SUCCESS of nationalist movements in gaining independence, and in many cases defeating local communist parties in the process, forced the Soviet Union by 1954 to accept that independence could be achieved under the leadership of the national bourgeoisie rather than the proletariat and to adopt a more subtle strategy of indirect approach in order to increase Russian influence and the prospects of an eventual communist take-over. Although nationalist parties might be socialist and neutralist and therefore suitable for a temporary alliance and for communist co-operation, they were not to be regarded as the final solution. One of the best examples of this has been the Russian support for President Nasser even though the Egyptian Government has been consistently anti-communist in its domestic policy. It is the Russian view that in the end only the proletariat can achieve the final liberation of such countries as Egypt through a social revolution. Khrushchev summed this up at the 21st Party Congress in early 1959 when he said: "After the colonisers have been driven out and when the national tasks have been mainly solved, the people seek an answer to the social problems advanced."

From the Russian point of view, therefore, it was not necessary that the communist party should be in the vanguard during the initial stages of revolution. In conformity with this line, during the period of co-existence after 1954, there occurred two important revolutionary wars in Algeria and Cuba which were not led by the communist party and in which neither Russia nor China played a prominent role. These two wars were, however, subsequently to have a profound effect in furthering the communist cause and in opening up both Africa and Latin America to communist subversion and penetration.

The French had hardly recovered from their defeat in Indo-China when on 1 November, 1954, the revolution broke out in Algeria. They were caught by surprise for the simple and familiar reason that they had six different and competing intelligence agencies responsible for assessing and countering the threat. In the first outbreak seventy separate attacks and incidents occurred, chiefly in the Aurès mountains. The attacks were soon extended to the Kabylia mountain area on the coast. The French made the initial mistake (as happened in Greece) of concentrating their effort on these enemy base areas with the result that, although through the establishment of pacification zones some control of the Aurès area was regained, the war spread right through Algeria to the western frontier with Morocco, and the city of Algiers itself became a hot-bed of terrorism. Not until 12 March, 1956, when the French National Assembly passed the Special Powers Act and the forces in Algeria, originally some 50,000, were raised to over 400,000, did the French really get down to it. Profiting from their experience in Indo-China and the trial pacification zones in the Aurès mountains, Special Administrative Sections (SAS) were set up to extend the zones to all areas. Between one and two million people in the rural areas were re-grouped for purposes of control and protection, and local defence forces over 100,000 strong were raised. (The French had learned the lesson, which the United States did not learn, that the alternative to re-groupment is refugees flooding

into the outskirts of neighbouring towns and making
them in turn more difficult to protect and control.)
The guerrilla units within Algeria were gradually
broken up and isolated. The National Liberation
Front (FLN) was forced to establish its bases outside
Algeria in Tunisia and Morocco, both independent
since 1956, instead of, as initially, inside the country.
To deal with this, the French built the Morice Line
along the Tunisian frontier for 250 miles from Bône
to the Sahara, manned on the average by 100 men a
mile. In such open terrain this barrier, though expensive, proved effective and by 1960 the French
had to all intents and purposes won the military war.
They had, however, neglected, as in Indo-China, to
propose a credible alternative political solution and
thus had no political aim.

It was this lack of an acceptable alternative political solution which made it impossible for the French
to retain control of the many Muslim leaders and
forces which had rallied to their cause against the
FLN. As soon as such groups, armed and equipped
by the French, gained military control of an area,
they immediately clashed with the French on the
question of political and administrative control. The
case of the "South Algerian Commandos" under
Mohamed Bellounis is a good example. As soon
as this group regained military control in the Atlas
mountain area from the FLN, it immediately exercised
political and administrative control and proposed
to the French that its zone of action should be
extended to the whole of Algeria with the result
that there were soon clashes between them, and
the commandos rapidly disintegrated. Out of a group

of over 3,000 only 300 finally remained with the French.

The original French political aim had been the integration of Algeria into metropolitan France but the thought of more than ten million Algerians being in a position to flood the home labour market was too much for any French Government to tolerate. When the Fourth Republic fell and General de Gaulle returned to power, he opened negotiations with the FLN for a fresh political solution. From that moment it became clear that France, although militarily in control, was wobbling politically, and the entire Muslim population almost overnight went over to the FLN.

One of the chief reasons for the failure of revolutionary wars in Greece, Malaya and the Philippines was the existence or promotion of an alternative political solution to that of the revolutionary movement. The French Government failed to find such a solution both in Indo-China and Algeria. One side-effect of this was that the failure on the political front brought the French army into the national political arena, nearly leading to civil war in France.

The French doctrine towards revolutionary war needs to be carefully considered and analysed because it was based on extensive experience in both Indo-China and Algeria. It was their view that such wars were all part of a protracted conflict designed to destroy the West through indirect but in the end decisive military action, thus avoiding any resort either to conventional or nuclear war. This to them did not mean that either Russia or China would overtly support such wars but that, if such support was not evident in the early stages of the war or even during the course of the war, their presence would become apparent later. Winning or losing one such war would be of little account. It would be the whole series which would matter. This would inevitably create a trend in the West either to contain the threat by becoming directly involved or to retreat in front of it, letting one area after another go. They deprecated the general Western view which accepted the nuclear deterrent and also paid more attention to limited war in the conventional sense, while looking on revolutionary wars merely as occasional incidents, whereas to the French these were of paramount importance. The form of war, or the type of weapons used, was irrelevant because whereas a nuclear bomb might be in a general and impersonal sense ultimate, a knife or a clonk on the head was equally ultimate in the individual sense. It was the purpose of the war which counted and to the French the overall aim of revolutionary war was to weaken the West to the advantage of the communist powers.*

The validity of the argument can hardly be disputed, but the French drew two unfortunate conclusions. The first was that, because the communist theory of revolutionary war worked so well, therefore counter-revolutionary war must be based on the same techniques. To a certain extent this is

---

* Professor C. Northcote Parkinson has supported this argument in characteristic terms: "Should they ever turn from science fiction to fact, the politicians would see that their world can be destroyed piece-meal, and has been very largely destroyed already, without anyone resorting to anything much larger than a 3 in. mortar."

true in that order and control have to be restored by detailed, determined and often repressive measures. When these are left almost entirely in the hands of military or police forces, without adequate civilian control working for an eventual political solution, there will be an excess of force and brutality. The population may be controlled but it will not be won. This will mean that such control has to be permanent instead of merely holding the ring while a political solution is found. Where the control is dependent on a foreign presence, the population will temporarily bow to it but will realise that, in the long run, it will have to bow to the stronger local presence. (This has been exactly the situation in the South Korean areas of responsibility in South Vietnam.) The techniques and theory of counter-revolutionary war are in fact only effective within the framework of a political solution which will in the end win and retain the voluntary political support of a good majority of the population.

Arising from this the other unfortunate conclusion drawn by the French was that threatened territories must be held militarily by the West to prevent them falling into communist hands, thereby dividing the world into the equivalent of two military camps. This again is an imitation of communist practice. It was tantamount to saying that, just as Russia must use its army to hold Czechoslovakia, so must the West in the same way hold the countries of the Third World. The French doctrine, developed by the army, led to defeat in Algeria and was nearly disastrous for France herself.

The FLN in Algeria was basically a nationalist,

not a communist, movement. The Vietminh were, however, much admired by the FLN for their victory at Dien Bien Phu and the revolutionary war theories of Mao provided the basic strategy and tactics. Apart from that the FLN, in accordance with Chinese teaching, had to be self-reliant. Russia could not accord any recognition to the FLN because of her own relationship with the French Government (national interest again taking precedence over ideo-logy), but China recognised the FLN's "Provisional Government of the Algerian Republic" in 1958. Subsequently, after independence, both countries were able to extend their influence in Algeria, with Russia recognising what the West, in spite of its World War II experience, has been inclined to forget, that control of the North African coast presents a real threat to the southern flank of Europe. While Russia extended her influence through trade and aid and the provision of arms, China was more interested in Algeria as a base for revolutionary support of other areas in Africa and provided funds and instructors for a guerrilla warfare school at Tlemcen, which be-came a powerful centre for the training of "freedom fighters" from many African countries. "The second scramble for Africa", as President Nyerere of Tan-zania was to call it later, was about to begin.

The situation within many African States immedi-ately after gaining independence seemed to offer ripe opportunities for subversion and intrigue, none more so than in the tragic case of the former Belgian Congo in 1960. Whereas in former British and French colonial territories in Africa moderate nationalist governments had succeeded to power and could maintain their position against the threats of outside subversion or internal disorder with limited Western support (which included the use of British troops to quell the East African mutinies), the situation in the Congo became immediately chaotic when the new State's Belgian-trained army mutinied. This provided the Soviet Union with an opportunity to air-lift supplies and agents to support the Prime Minister, Patrice Lumumba, while Soviet and Czech Embassy personnel in the capital of Leopoldville (now Kinshasa) rose to over 200. This intervention was short-lived with the dismissal of Lumumba by the President and the succession to power of Colonel (later General) Mobutu who gave the communist embassies forty hours to leave the country. Russia then attempted a backdoor entry through Stanleyville in support of Gizenga who claimed the succession to Lumumba. This achieved a temporary success, when Gizenga became Deputy Premier in Adoula's government in 1961, but he soon broke away back to Stanleyville where he was supported by Russian arms and supplies, while Russia herself continued to maintain her embassy in Leopoldville, only to be expelled once again. The Russians then supported a Congolese government-in-exile at Brazzaville under Mulele, a former colleague of Lumumba. The turmoil within the Congo continued with the rise and fall of Tshombe. In the end United Nations forces, which had been called in to maintain law and order, had to be used to restore the unity of the State.

Russia was not alone in its meddling. The Chinese, Algerian, Egyptians and one or two other African States were also involved in the running of arms and the training and insertion of agents and small guerrilla forces, not just to the Congo. The Chinese were particularly active in Burundi by the end of 1963 with a large embassy whose task was to support the rebels in the Congo and in Rwanda and to subvert Burundi itself. Mao Tse-tung is reported by a Chinese defector to have said that "Burundi is the way to the Congo and, when the Congo falls, the whole of Africa will follow." Here again, after much skulduggery, which included the murder of the Prime Minister in 1965, the Chinese Embassy was evicted. Similar evictions occurred about the same time in a number of former French territories in Central Africa. Even Cuba became involved and scored one success when about twenty Africans trained in Cuba led the revolt in Zanzibar in January, 1964, in which Chinese-trained agents were also implicated. The subsequent union between Tanganyika and Zanzibar to form the Republic of Tanzania under President Nyerere, together with the suppression of almost simultaneous army mutinies in Tanganyika, Uganda and Kenya, prevented any outright communist success. Finally, the overthrow of President Nkrumah in Ghana, whose pan-African ambitions were supported by the communist powers, put a temporary end to the immediate communist hope, expressed by Chou En-lai when he said during a visit in 1965 that Africa was ripe for revolution, of establishing any communist State or enclave in the immediate aftermath of the granting of independence to African territories.

While the details in any one particular African country have been confused and complicated, the general pattern has been clear. Using all means and every opportunity irrespective of ideology both communist powers, together with their satellites, have conducted a persistent if not a concerted effort to support every form of rebel in the hope that one or more African States would be taken over by a revolutionary movement which, if not initially communist, would soon come under the control of a communist party and become dependent on the external support of one of the communist powers. It was not concerted because by this time Russia and China were rivals. There was also a difference in their methods. The Russians tended to maintain relations with moderate and even military governments, using the instrument of trade and aid, although surreptitiously supplying arms to and training agents for particular rebel groups which adhered to the Moscow line, while the Chinese, Cubans and others indulged in underground intrigue and subversion. As Dr Banda of Malawi put it in respect of Communist China in 1964: "Although their own people have not enough to eat, they find enough money to corrupt African politicians everywhere." Other African leaders also showed that the turmoil of the early 1960s had put Africa on its guard. President Nyerere was to say that "at no time shall we lower our guard against the subversion of our government or people" and the Kenya Government stated that it intended "to avert all revolutions, irrespective of their origins or whether they come from inside or are influenced from outside". The more direct assault having failed, there was after 1965 a significant change in the strategy.

The "freedom fighter" entered the lists and the target of the attack was ostensibly switched to the white countries of Southern Africa—the Portuguese colonies of Angola and Mozambique (and Guinea in West Africa), Rhodesia, South-West Africa and South Africa. These seemed to provide a promising opportunity to apply the theory and techniques of revolutionary war to the African continent. Whereas in the previous period in the African territories the various rebel groups, including those with communist affiliations, had little more of a cause than their own desire for power, in Southern Africa there was the combined cause of anti-colonialism, nationalism and racialism. On the other hand, the exponents of revolutionary war were up against well established, powerful and efficient governments. It might have been expected that, within a short period, the resultant conflicts would present a fairly clear picture, but in fact after four years the situation in all these territories is still confused.

The various liberation movements are reported to have between 20,000 and 30,000 trained guerrillas under arms in camps from Algeria to Zambia, with more in training in Russia, China and Cuba. Those nearer the "front" are secretly deployed within or on the borders of Angola, Rhodesia and Mozambique and in both Congoes, Zambia and Tanzania. The various controlling and supporting agencies seem to be scattered round the world, including London and New York, but with the greatest concentration in Dar-es-Salaam, Brazzaville and Kinshasa. The movements themselves are divided, factious and quarrelsome so that the issue is far from being a simple one of black Africa versus white Africa. African is still at loggerheads with African, just as Russia is with China in their support of the various movements.

The main groupings need only be briefly described. The most successful group in northern Mozambique is Frelimo, whose leader, Mr Mondlane, was recently murdered in Dar-es-Salaam. Operating from Tanzania it exercises some control in the northern provinces and has kept large-scale Portuguese forces fully occupied. Its main support is believed to come from Russia and Algeria. A dissident group named Coremo is also operating in the area. In Angola, the Portuguese colony on the west coast, there are three movements —the Popular Liberation Movement (MPLA), predominantly Marxist and operating from Zambia with Russian and Algerian support; GRAE, led by Mr Holden Roberto, claiming to be an Angolan government-in-exile, operating from Congo (Kinshasa) with Chinese and some covert American support; and Unita, recently expelled from Zambia for cutting the Benguela railway, and operating within Angola with reputedly Chinese support. In Rhodesia there are two—the Zimbabwe African People's Union, aided by Russia, Algeria and Cuba, and the Zimbabwe African National Union, supported by China, the former operating through Zambia from Tanzania and the latter in the south-east section of Rhodesia. In South-West Africa, the People's Organisation (SWAPO) operates along the northern border with Angola with sanctuaries in Zambia and support from the Angolan MPLA (i.e. Russian). China's counterpart is thought to be extinct. In South Africa there are also two—the African National Congress with

Russian support and the Pan-African Congress with Chinese support. Except for Frelimo in northern Mozambique, none of these groups control any territory within the threatened countries, even within the accepted revolutionary war meaning of the term, i.e. to the extent that they obtain any realistic local African support, supplies or recruits. The Organisation for African Unity, in so far as it has accepted the role, has failed to achieve any cohesive effort. The Russians now deal direct with the various movements which they support and there are indications, from a conference in Khartoum in January, 1969, that they are attempting to by-pass the OAU, to establish their own organisation for co-ordinating the various liberation movements, and to set up, in support of the guerrillas, a force containing regular units from other African States.

To meet the threat the Portuguese have adopted counter-revolutionary warfare techniques adapted from previous revolutionary wars, including the re-grouping of villages and organising of local defence forces. The efforts of the three threatened governments concerned have been well co-ordinated and South African police and military assistance has been provided to the other two. Their campaign has not been restricted to purely military and internal security measures. Although their political attitude towards Africans in their territories is to be condemned, their economic and social programmes, with improved material well-being, are not matched by those in other African territories. One consequence of this is that, while some recruits can be encouraged to leave the territories for training outside, the guerrilla bands which return, mainly on raids, generally obtain little assistance from the local population and in many cases are given away. The very fact that they operate from outside the territories with unmistakable outside support puts them into the position of being an invader or infiltrator rather than an insurgent. The local African therefore tends to defend his own territory against them.

The view expressed by Professor Ardrey in his book *The Territorial Imperative* that, if South Africa was invaded by a white nation, 80 per cent of the Africans would support South Africa, and that, if it was invaded by Africans, almost 100 per cent would support South Africa, cannot be entirely discounted. The point here is that the cause of nationalism is not operating in favour of the liberation movements, while the causes of anti-colonialism and racialism are ineffective, or at least considerably reduced, by the measures taken by the threatened governments. The tragedy therefore is that, if the liberation movements are going to launch a revolutionary war, their initial attack will have to be against the Africans in the threatened territories, using the most brutal and ruthless terrorism to compel their support or at least their neutrality. Without this, attacks on government forces and white settlers will get them nowhere.

The measures taken by the threatened governments are not confined within their own territories. There is a strong political and economic counter-offensive being mounted, mainly by South Africa. In many respects the governments, such as Congo (Kinshasa) and Zambia, are economically dependent at least for some facilities on the threatened governments. For example, guerrilla attacks on the Benguela railway, which carries Zambian and Congolese copper through Angola to the coast, are condemned by both governments. Moreover, the booming economy of South Africa has as much to offer most of the central African States as other foreign support. Finally, too overt support for the guerrillas by African governments could attract military retaliation, and this encourages an element of caution. The threat of such retaliation, however, is likely to be more compelling than the act (compare the bombing of North Vietnam).

The prospect, therefore, of another Vietnam, or anything like it, in central or southern Africa is very remote in the next few years. Violence will continue and the number of incidents may increase in a wave-like motion, depending on the amount of outside support, the co-ordination of effort and the repercussions of a possible American failure in Vietnam, but not to the extent that an explosive revolutionary war will erupt against the threatened governments. The "terrain" in every sense is not yet suitable. A likely, and more dangerous, outcome is that the liberation movements, having failed, may then backfire and overthrow one or two of the central African governments which now support and harbour them.

Although, from the communist point of view, this ambivalent strategy (encouraging liberation movements to attack the more popular and attractive outside target of the white governments in southern Africa) may fail in its purpose, it should at least have the effect, because of the label of respectability which it gives to communist aid and support, of increasing their influence and penetration in central Africa, thereby creating opportunities for subsequent communist take-overs there, particularly if moderate central African governments can be blamed for the failure through their own caution.* For Russia it is an ideal can-win can't-lose strategy with a low risk of confrontation.

There are many who regard the case of Cuba as an example of a successful rebellion rather than a successful revolutionary war, partly because the communist party was not in control of the revolution during the course of the war and partly because the form and phases of the fighting seemed inconsistent with the orthodox theory. To a certain extent it was a Russian two-stage revolution where the rebels under Fidel Castro won the war between December, 1956, and January, 1959, and afterwards, discovering that they were really Marxists, established a communist government in Cuba in December, 1961. Otherwise, on balance, it must qualify as a revolutionary war because it was a revolution, not just to overthrow the government of President Batista and to seize power, but to effect completely radical changes in both the government and the social structure of the country. Certainly it was the most inefficient example of a successful revolutionary war but it was also up against an equally, if not more, inefficient government. The result of this was that the war did not have to go through the normal three phases because

* This process seems to be happening in the Lebanon where a moderate government is threatened by revolutionary forces.

victory was achieved and the government collapsed under the threat of comparatively low-scale guerrilla warfare. The cause of the revolutionaries was so good, as compared with that of the Batista government, that neither their organisation nor their techniques had to be as sophisticated as those in other examples. The majority of the rural population was on the side of the revolutionaries and did not have to be coerced. This meant that the revolutionaries received very good intelligence and could depend for supplies on the local population. Most of the arms were captured from the government forces and it is estimated that only about 15 per cent were smuggled in, mainly in small consignments from the United States. Because of the inefficiency of the government and the low morale of its forces, the guerrillas did not have to pay dearly for their own mistakes. Their training and experience were very low in comparison with the Vietcong. Tactics, marksmanship and fire control were so poor that the expenditure of ammunition, of which there is always inclined to be a shortage in revolutionary war, was prodigal. The terrain, however, was favourable and offensive operations could be carried out always with surprise and with little risk. Few attacks were pressed and hardly any defensive operations had to be fought. If attacked the guerrillas simply disappeared. A novel measure adopted by the revolutionaries was to disarm all prisoners and to return them, after a scathing lecture, to the government through the Cuban Red Cross without any form of parole or duress. This utter contempt for the government forces still further lowered their morale. By the end of the campaign the revolutionary forces had no large units (they were not required for phase three) and were estimated to number only about 15,000.

The theoretician of the war was Che Guevara, who reproduced three Maoist conclusions from his Cuba experience: that the forces of the people could win a war against an army; that it was not necessary to wait for the fulfilment of all conditions for a revolution because the focus of insurrection would create them; and that the area for the armed struggle in under-developed Latin America was the rural countryside.

The first of these has been proved true provided that the revolutionaries have a basic cause, a sound organisation, a suitable terrain and other favourable factors. In his thesis Che Guevara repeats very closely the theory of Mao Tse-tung, with emphasis on the quotation: "All guiding principles in military operations proceed without exception from one basic principle, that is to strive as far as possible to preserve one's own strength and annihilate that of the enemy." He covers the type of warfare to be fought both in suitable terrain and in unfavourable terrain, such as in well developed heavily populated plains with little cover and also in suburban areas. He makes the good point that "the ideal prey is the enemy in movement" and stresses that fire should be concentrated on the advance guard so that troops refuse to occupy this position. There is nothing very novel in his manual but he himself was to prove incapable of practising what Mao had preached and he had learnt.

His other two conclusions, however, are not

necessarily valid. Only if the organisation of the
revolutionary movement is sound and certain conditions of "terrain" are present will a revolution itself
produce sufficient tension to create the further
conditions necessary for success. Revolutions can after
all be premature. It is also doubtful whether the area
for the armed struggle in Latin America is the rural
countryside. Che Guevara's belief in these two conclusions, coupled with a failure to follow his own
theories, was to cost him his life in Bolivia when he
tried to extend the Cuban revolution to Continental
Latin America.

The initial interesting effect of the Cuban revolution and of the rise of a new communist government
to power was the complete breakdown of the Cuban
economy which necessitated massive economic support from the Soviet Union. It has been an extremely
expensive operation for the Russians and is yet
another reason for Russian reluctance to support
revolutionary war in cases where this might be one
of the results. Russian resources, and the capacity to
distribute them, do not compare with those of the
United States. Cuba, and later Vietnam, have
demonstrated that, on a world-wide scale, it is far
easier for the United States to support threatened
governments than it is for Russia to support
revolutionaries, even successful ones. It was not only
economic support which Cuba required but also
political and military, because there was still the
threat that the United States might support a
counter-revolution, even after the failure of the Bay
of Pigs, or herself invade Cuba. This threat was
relieved by Russia as a result of the Cuban missile

crisis. Khrushchev may have been compelled by President Kennedy to withdraw the nuclear missiles and to destroy their launching sites, but in return he did achieve an important political success in obtaining a firm undertaking from the President that the United States would not invade Cuba. The permanency of the revolution was thereby secured and Cuba became another centre for the export of revolution.

Its zeal and fervour in this respect were not, however, matched by its expertise. The aim was to create "new Vietnams" in Latin America, not only as a means of subverting Latin-American States and establishing communist governments in them, but in order to involve the United States and thereby stretch her economy and resources to the utmost. This was the intention behind Che Guevara's adventure in Bolivia. It was not just to overthrow the Bolivian Government but to create a movement which would become the focus for revolution in the whole of the continent and so to liberate this "countryside area" of the world from the "city" imperialism of the United States. A Dominican follower of Castro summed it up as follows: "From my conversations with the world's top communist leaders, I arrived at the inevitable, and not strange, conclusion that Latin America constitutes the fundamental means for reaching the United States."

The terrain in Latin America in every sense seemed eminently suitable for revolutionary war. Topographically it was ideal and politically, socially and economically all the necessary ingredients appeared to be present. Most of the governments were ineffective and unstable while some were military and oppressive. None seemed capable of carrying out the reforms necessary to give their countries political stability or economic development. The remedies proposed in President Kennedy's Alliance for Progress had had little effect. The annual economic growth rate remained as low as 1·5 per cent. Income distribution had the greatest disparity of any area in the world, while only half the children went to school and only 5 per cent received any higher education. Owing to the fall in the market price of primary products, the Latin-American share in world trade had dropped from 11 to 5 per cent in less than fifteen years. American aid of $6 billion between 1961–6 made little impact because, as the Latin-American governments complained, they had repaid more than twice that sum in interest, loan repayments and remitted profits during the same period. It was against this background in April, 1967, that Che Guevara issued his call for "new Vietnams" throughout the continent.

Minor insurgencies had already been simmering for many years in several of the territories and in the previous few years there had been a dozen *coups d'état*, yet now in 1969, almost two years since Che Guevara's adventure and death in Bolivia, there is no sign of a new Vietnam. In Bolivia itself certainly anything might still happen. A combination of students, miners and disgruntled military elements might stage a revolt which could lead to a communist victory, but in no sense would it be a true revolutionary war. In Argentina there have been minor guerrilla incidents which, in spite of a communist-

Peronist alliance and an oppressive military dictatorship, have easily been kept in check by the military.
Much the same situation prevails in Brazil except that
a new communist party (*Accão Nacional*) has been
formed and is concentrating on political activity as a
pre-requisite for the armed struggle. It could have
some success, in combination with the outlawed
National Students' Union, by continuing to rob
banks and stage demonstrations and by increasing
urban terrorism.* Only in Venezuela much earlier,
in 1962, had there been a near-success when the
liberation movement (FALN), supported by the
communist party, attracted sufficient of the student
youth in Caracas to launch an outbreak of urban
terrorism combined with guerrilla activity in the
countryside. But the measures taken by Presidents
Betancourt and Leoni over the next few years,
including social and agrarian reforms, coupled with
the efficiency and loyalty of the armed forces, now
seem to have reduced the threat to negligible propor-
tions. In much the same way the guerrilla threat in
both Colombia and Peru, which was at one time
serious, has also been greatly reduced. Only in
Guatemala, where it is the army that has broken up
into factions and where no social and economic reforms have been initiated, does the threat remain—
at least of a civil war which might provoke American
intervention.

The prospect, therefore, of revolutionary wars in
Latin America on the Cuban or communist model is
remote. Communism as a revolutionary force, whether
from Moscow or Peking, has been losing ground,

* And by kidnapping ambassadors.

while Cuba itself is not exactly a shining star which others wish to emulate. Added to this, the failure of Che Guevara and Castro's support for the Russian invasion of Czechoslovakia have discredited the communist export model of revolution. The tendency in Latin America is more towards an indigenous form of revolution, which is likely to combine idealistic young officers in the forces, very different from the earlier more conservative power seekers, dissident and reforming priests of the Catholic Church and students, willing to riot and demonstrate, but not to suffer the rigours of insurgency, on the Nasser rather than the Castro pattern.

The part played by China in all this has been negligible, while Russia has been faced with the usual dilemma arising from a conflict between ideological and national interests. For example, at the first Tri-Continental Solidarity Conference held at Havana in 1966, the Russian delegation which naturally had to subscribe to all the revolutionary resolutions passed at the conference,* was disowned by the Russian government as unofficial when Latin-American governments, with which Russia had diplomatic relations, protested. The Soviet Union has tried to chart its course so as to retain control over the orthodox communist parties in competition with Peking, to pay lip service to revolutionary war, while preventing any Castro adventure from getting out of control, to maintain normal relations with Latin-American States and to avoid a direct confrontation with the United States.

* The normal method of communication between communist parties. In this case it probably gave the signal to Che Guevara to create new Vietnams.

In the long term, Russia as a means of extending her influence can be expected to support with trade and aid any new Nasser-type government which may arise, relying less on communist coups or revolutionary war, but rather on a gradual two-stage revolution, while encouraging anti-American demonstrations and supporting a steady propaganda attack against the "*Yanquis*" to reduce American influence.

Russia would therefore appear to be adopting, on a world-wide basis, a more indirect and cautious strategic approach. She is well aware that, if and when a revolution is successful in any country in the Third World, she will have to support it, probably at long range and certainly at some expense. The tentacles must, therefore, be well established first through trade and aid, followed by the flag, initially into the Mediterranean, the Persian Gulf and the Indian Ocean. This new approach requires that normal relations and co-operation should be maintained with existing governments and that revolutionary forces should only be openly supported if their target is not the local government but something external, for example, in the Middle East Israel, in Africa white South Africa, and in Latin America American imperialism. This approach holds out the best prospect of uniting the many revolutionary forces in the various regions against a common target without alarming, but instead disarming, local national governments. As an instrument of policy revolutionary war remains available, but only where its success seems to be assured and where the effort of waging it would not be counter-productive.

China, on the other hand, is prepared to support

revolutionary forces in the Third World against existing non-communist governments and to advocate revolutionary war on the Chinese model as the best method of advancing world revolution and the expansion of communist influence and control. In taking this line, she is in direct rivalry with Russia and has not hesitated to use even racialist arguments to support her bid for leadership of the revolutionary forces by identifying Russia with the West and therefore the whites. This came through very clearly at the time of the proposed Afro-Asian Solidarity Conference in Algiers where China's whole effort was directed towards excluding the Russians. In so far as the two communist strategic approaches react on each other in support of revolutionary forces, Russia is being compelled by Chinese criticism to increase the level of aid while China is under pressure from Russia to reduce the pace and, with it, the risk.

Which approach will prevail and what course events may take will depend very largely on the outcome of the Vietnam war, which in all respects has been a test case, not just between East and West, but between the rival strategies of Russia and China, in addition to being the supreme example of revolutionary war at its most sophisticated and savage.

7

Vietnam

SCORES of books and thousands of articles, not to mention television interviews, have been produced on Vietnam and more are still to come. It cannot be expected, therefore, that in one short chapter I can give a blow by blow account of the war itself from 1959 to 1969. It will, however, be necessary to pick out certain highlights in order to show the part played by the war in world strategy affecting, as it has, the policies of all major powers and the emotions and opinions of nearly all people.

It should come as no surprise that a war, which was to be fought so close to the birth-place of revolutionary war and in an arena where one successful revolutionary war had already been fought, should develop the art of such wars to their highest degree of refinement. The prophets, priests and chairmen were themselves closely involved, and the local terrain in every sense —topographical, demographical, political, social and economic—was eminently suitable. The people themselves on both sides were politically highly conscious and active with a long tradition of war and violence. At the same time South Vietnam was lacking in the government institutions and administrative structure which might have given it some cohesion as a country and helped to maintain law, order and a measure of stability. The economy and population were such that there was a surplus of both resources and energy, two essential factors for waging revolutionary war at a high scale of intensity. Many countries were to become involved on one side or the other, with the communist powers supporting and supplying North Vietnam and the Vietcong, and most Western powers and many neighbouring Asian countries supporting

South Vietnam in one way or another. As was to be expected, therefore, the war in Vietnam became a test case for revolutionary war as between East and West. It has also become a theatre for Russian-Chinese rivalry. When it is all over, it will undoubtedly prove to be one of the decisive wars of this century and, in its influence, more far-reaching than any other war of its type, even that in China itself. Already at the end of the 1960s it has had more divisive results on world opinion than the Spanish Civil War of the 1930s and its real effects are still to come.

The Geneva Agreement of 1954 relating to Vietnam achieved only two results—the signing of a cease-fire and the technical surrender of French sovereignty. Temporarily there was a *de facto* partition of Vietnam at the 17th Parallel with neither the government in Hanoi nor that in Saigon agreeing to this as a permanent solution. Both regarded themselves as successors to the French in Vietnam, and moreover the communists in the North, under their Vietminh label, regarded themselves as successors to the French in the whole of Indo-China through the Pathet-Lao and Khmer Issarak off-shoots of their party organisation. These last claims they were forced to abandon at Geneva, because Russia and China were not prepared to press them, so that the independent governments and countries of Laos and Cambodia were established under separate Agreements. The basic division of Vietnam into two parts was openly demonstrated when, under the provisions of the Agreement, people on both sides of the dividing line were allowed to decide in which half they preferred to live. Nearly one million people, comprising whole communities and families, the majority of them Catholic, left their homes in the North and moved to the South. There is strong evidence that this figure would have been considerably higher if more transport facilities had been available, if the time limit of 300 days had been extended, and if contact could have been made with those wishing to leave by teams from the International Control Commission. In the opposite direction well under 100,000 moved to the North, the majority of them being young men who had served in the Vietminh forces. Many of these were hastily married before departure, and had to leave their new wives behind, as a means of strengthening and maintaining their family link with their native villages. This majority movement of refugees from north to south (voting with their feet) provides fair evidence that the population, while wanting the French out, did not necessarily want Ho Chi Minh in. President Eisenhower was undoubtedly correct when he stated at this time that in a straight vote between Ho Chi Minh and the ex-Emperor Bao Dai, Head of State in the French-established Vietnamese government, 80 per cent of the population would have voted for Ho Chi Minh. The question was whether or not a credible and more acceptable alternative to both of them would appear in the South. The only figure of any national stature, untainted by co-operation with either the communists or the French, was Ngo Dinh Diem who first became Prime Minister and then, in 1955, President of the Republic of Vietnam. The vote within South Vietnam in favour of establishing a separate republic under his Presidency was overwhelming. Quite unnecessary manipulation pushed

it to over ninety-nine per cent but, without it, Diem
would still have had a very substantial majority.

It was this referendum, coupled with the specific
opposition of the South Vietnamese representatives
at the Geneva Conference to the clause in the un-
signed Final Declaration providing for elections in
1956 (to decide on the reunification of North and
South), which enabled the new government to refuse
compliance with this provision. They had two further
reasons for such refusal, the first being that the voting
in the North, even if internationally supervised, could
not have been free, because of intimidation by the
party, and the second being that the North, because
of its greater numbers by some millions, could have
out-voted the South, whose people would not therefore
have been given a free choice. The Geneva Conference
having failed to settle the question of reunification,
it is now being decided by force through the
instrument of revolutionary war.

The French, while their expeditionary force still
remained in South Vietnam, made one last attempt
to regain their influence by plotting with supporters
of Bao Dai for the overthrow of Diem, but his position, with strong American support, was too secure
and the attempt failed. There can be little doubt that,
if it had succeeded, South Vietnam would either have
rapidly collapsed (which the communists had expected
in the post-Geneva period) or a deal would have been
made with the North leading to the reunification of
the country under a communist government. Although there would have been no second Vietnam
war, it is impossible to speculate what might then
have happened in South East Asia over the last fifteen

years. As it was, the immediate departure of the French expeditionary force was demanded and French influence rapidly declined. This, however, was not to prevent them from intriguing, as a matter of pique as much as of policy, against subsequent South Vietnamese governments and the United States.

With the departure of the French, Diem requested and received from President Eisenhower both aid and military assistance. United States general policy had already been declared by John Foster Dulles in March, 1954, before the Geneva Agreements, in the following terms:

> Under the conditions of today, the imposition on South East Asia of the political system of communist Russia and its Chinese communist ally by whatever means would be a grave threat to the whole free community. The United States feels that that possibility should not be passively accepted but should be met by united action. This might involve serious risks but these risks are far less than those that will face us a few years from now if we dare not be resolute today. . . . The chances for peace are usually bettered by letting a potential aggressor know in advance where his aggression could lead him.

To all intents and purposes the Truman Doctrine was being extended to South East Asia and the 17th Parallel was selected as the stop-line. The Treaty of Manila and the establishment of SEATO* followed to give collective effect to this.

As a result of Geneva, Russia had secured the

* South East Asia Treaty Organisation.

creation of a new communist State, the first since Czechoslovakia in 1948, and at least temporary stability in the Far East, with cease-fires both in Korea and Indo-China, which was to stand her in good stead during the troubles on her southern front later in 1956. China had also secured a friendly and grateful neighbour covering the access routes to her southern front. The co-chairmanship (with Britain) of the Geneva Conference did not prevent Russia providing both political and economic assistance to North Vietnam in conjunction with China. Both supported the North Vietnamese demand for elections in 1956, but without great enthusiasm, because the same arguments could be adversely applied to Germany and Korea. There seemed no reason at this point why peace should not be kept on the basis of a cease-fire and partition at the 17th Parallel in much the same way as it was being kept, if somewhat uneasily, on the 38th Parallel in Korea and on the Berlin wall.

The initial problem facing President Diem in South Vietnam was to create and preserve the unity of the new State. In this he had some initial success by breaking the political and military power of the regional sects (the Binh Xuyen, the Cao Dai and the Hoa Hao) and by imposing government control over the army. Economic conditions in the South improved as compared with the North, where the communists' collectivisation programme led to revolts in Thanh Hoa and Nghe An provinces which were ruthlessly suppressed. It was even possible, in addition to the departure of the French Army, to reduce the size of the South Vietnamese forces by approximately 20,000 men, whereas in North Vietnam the original seven divisions of the Vietminh were expanded into the People's Army of Vietnam (PAVN) of twenty divisions.

The point was that the North could not indefinitely tolerate the division imposed by the Geneva Agreement nor the creation of a rival, and initially successful, Republic of Vietnam in the South. With reunification by elections barred and little prospect of a collapse in the South, a return to the "armed struggle" remained the only alternative. Overt invasion on the Korean model was clearly inadvisable. It would have neither Russian nor Chinese support and would attract an immediate American response with full Western support. The instrument of revolutionary war was, however, readily available. The former Vietminh underground organisation, though now threatened by the government of South Vietnam, was still intact in the South, while in the North there were more than 50,000 southerners trained and ready to be infiltrated back. Although the split between Russia and China had developed, with China becoming the leading advocate of revolutionary war as a means of defeating imperialism, Russia was at least ready to concur. The World Communist Declaration of 1960 endorsing national liberation movements was subscribed to by over eighty communist parties, including both Moscow and Peking. This signal confirmed to Hanoi that she could rely on the limited outside support necessary to wage a revolutionary war. In fact China alone could supply most of her initial elementary needs in rice and small-arms. Further delay would have been fatal by allowing the Diem regime to consolidate its position, to recover outlying rural areas, where there was still Vietminh control, and to continue the successful economic development of the South. Incidents, mainly of a terrorist nature and consistent with phase one of revolutionary war, including the murder of village headmen and local officials, had started in 1957 and 1958. By 1959 small-scale guerrilla actions were erupting in the Mekong Delta. By 1961 the war was well into phase two throughout the whole of the South.

Within the space of six years between 1959 and 1965 the Vietcong, supported and directed by North Vietnam, had defeated the people and government of South Vietnam and were poised to take the country over as it collapsed. It was a classical campaign waged in accordance with orthodox communist teaching against a government which was fully alive to the threat and a people who were prepared to suffer great hardships and heavy casualties to prevent a communist take-over. They were supported by the political, military and economic might of the United States. On the one side it was an impressive victory and on the other a dismal defeat.

Although at the start there were factors in the situation favourable to both sides, the initial balance in armed strength, resources and popular support in the countryside was heavily in favour of the government. Fundamentally the issue was decided by organisation—by the capacity of the Vietcong to organise their revolutionary movement (as described in Chapter I) and at the same time to disrupt the government organisation, and by a complementary failure on the part of the government to organise itself effectively, thereby wasting its superior resources, and to disrupt the Vietcong organisation, especially the political underground organisation within the population. The weak link in the whole of the government structure was the administrative contact between the central government, including its various departments, and the villages. Not only did the government fail to improve on what was left by the French (in terms of administrative services, trained officials and ground communications) but the Vietcong were able in all the outlying areas of the countryside to cut this link and keep it cut, so that villages were isolated and could be contacted by the government only through its military forces.

There was also an omission on the government's part to establish a firm security framework throughout the country based on a trained national police force with the army in mobile support. Instead of such a police force, there was a proliferation of local paramilitary forces, whose activities were unco-ordinated and frequently misdirected, with the result that the numerical superiority of the government was largely wasted. Rival intelligence organisations grew up so that the intelligence available to the government was both sketchy and unreliable. A large unwieldy army, organised, equipped and trained for conventional war, added to the confusion and waste. Its very size, attracting as it did most of the talented young men in the country, led to both a political and economic imbalance, so that the army became the fount of political power and a drain on the country's manpower and financial resources, and to a complete dependence on massive American aid, which in turn demoralised the country and corrupted its citizens.

The whole mess defied any system of rational control and, without that, it proved impossible to develop a winning strategy.

Instead, therefore, of one war—political, economic and military—being fought against the enemy, there were separate wars in all these fields multiplied by the administrative and military divisions within the country. Lacking both organisation and a system of control, the government was quite incapable of implementing any of the measures necessary at any given moment to deal with the situation. Performance was so erratic that many of the measures which might otherwise have worked proved counter-productive. There was a consequential inclination to copy communist methods, and all the mistakes of the previous campaigns elsewhere were repeated (such as, for example, an emphasis on military operations against enemy bases in the remoter areas of the country instead of on securing the developed and populated areas). To all this confusion the United States, having learned few of the lessons of previous campaigns, happily contributed to such an extent that the main function of the South Vietnamese government was soon confined to the absorption and expenditure of American aid.

Those measures adopted by the French in Algeria, including regroupment of the outlying population and the establishment of pacification zones, might have worked because, in South Vietnam, there was an alternative political solution already present but, under rising pressure, this too was soon to collapse with the fall of Diem. When the inevitable threat to the unity of the state developed, South Vietnam's

American-type Constitution, which with its many
checks and balances only just works in the United
States, could not cope with emergency conditions
where the executive had to exercise overriding powers.
The authoritarian rule of President Diem, by no
means as harsh as that of many other heads of State
around the world, was thus exposed to its critics and
enemies. His own personal failure lay, not in loss
of popular support in the countryside or loss of contact with the people, but in loss of control over the
sources of power, notably among the French-edu-
cated in the army and in the urban middle-class,
neither of whom had any better claim, in fact less, to
either popular support or contact with the people.
After his overthrow at the end of 1963, the collapse
of government authority accelerated. In addition to
military defeats and loss of control in the rural areas,
an alternative non-communist political solution had
temporarily ceased to be credible.

At Geneva in 1954 an Agreement had also been
signed establishing the independent kingdom of Laos
but leaving its northern provinces of Phong Saly and
Sam Neua under the control of the Pathet-Lao, themselves communist-controlled and in alliance with the
Vietminh. It was the Western hope at Geneva that
Laos would become a peaceful, neutral buffer State,
but its geographical position controlling all the mountain trails between China and North Vietnam on the
one hand and north east Thailand, Cambodia and
South Vietnam on the other, dictated that it would
instead become a battleground.* The communists

* Laos—Buffer State or Battleground, by Hugh Toye
(O.U.P., 1968).

were able to exploit the ethnic and political divisions of the country and by 1961 were threatening its complete take-over. To meet this threat, President Kennedy, with British and Australian approval, dispatched American marines to north east Thailand and greatly increased American military assistance to the Thais.

The prospect of a direct confrontation involving American combat troops was sufficient to cause the communist powers to hold back and to initiate a second Geneva Conference to discuss the future of Laos. Under the Geneva Agreement of 1962 a neutralist government was established in Laos with a coalition between the neutralists, the communists and the right wing. From this the communists were soon to withdraw, while retaining control in the northern provinces and also in the mountain jungles of the "pan-handle" along the Vietnamese border. While the Agreement ostensibly prevented open hostilities from breaking out in Laos, it in fact enabled the communists to achieve their two primary aims: first, the consolidation of the Pathet-Lao position from which, when the opportunity offered (for example, after an American withdrawal from South Vietnam), the remainder of Laos could be swallowed, and secondly, as a vital element in the Vietnam war, the securing of control over the sparsely populated mountain areas along the Vietnamese border, now popularly known as the Ho Chi Minh trail. The possibility of the Laotian Government regaining control of this area with the help of American forces had to be prevented at all costs. The only price which had to be paid was to allow a nominally independent Laotian Government to continue functioning in Vientiane for the time being.

Meanwhile, the situation in South East Asia generally seemed to be developing to communist advantage. Russian aid since 1955 and the sale of arms to Indonesia had paid off in 1963 with the "confrontation" against Malaysia, which had just been formed by a federation between independent Malaya and the three former British colonies of Singapore, Sarawak and North Borneo (Sabah). The Indonesian Communist Party under Aidit had fully recovered from the failure of 1948 and was now the third largest communist party in the world. It had successfully penetrated the Indonesian government and army and had great influence over President Sukarno. By focusing Indonesian attention on an outside enemy —Britain and Malaya—there was every chance that the revolutionary forces, represented by the communist party within Indonesia, would be able to seize power from the moderate forces represented by the leading generals in the army. The coup, however, when it came, failed and the excesses committed by the communist party during the attempt led to their ruthless extermination* by the surviving generals and to the fall of Sukarno. (The pattern of this attempted coup is one that could well be repeated elsewhere in the Middle East or central Africa in similar circumstances in the future.) As far as Malaysia was concerned, the threat was successfully met and all Indonesian raids into Malaysian territory were repulsed. The campaign provided a good example of a co-ordinated effort between a Western power and a

* Over 500,000 are estimated to have been killed.

small threatened territory and showed how, when emphasis is placed on maintaining control in the vital populated areas, guerrilla activity and infiltration can be defeated. Nevertheless, partly as a result of the tensions caused by "confrontation", Singapore seceded from Malaysia and became a separate State.

Elsewhere in South East Asia the dominoes were being lined up for the period after the eventual fall of South Vietnam. Huk dissidents remained in the Philippines and, in Malaya, the Malayan Communist Party continued operating underground with over 500 guerrillas under arms on the Malayan-Thai border. An incipient insurgency was promoted among the neglected Lao population of north east Thailand, where it could be supported by Pathet-Lao and North Vietnamese penetration through southern Laos across the Mekong. China, meanwhile, was also encouraging revolts among the ethnic hill tribe minorities in northern Thailand, Burma, Assam and the Himalays. She had already pre-empted her claim to southern Asia as her sphere of influence by the defeat of India in the border war at the end of 1962. All progress would, however, depend on the outcome in South Vietnam. This was to be the decisive war. As General Giap had proclaimed: "If we win here, we shall win everywhere."

By the beginning of 1965, South Vietnam was on the verge of collapse, in spite of massive American aid and the presence of more than 20,000 American advisers. When early in February, 1965, the bombing of North Vietnam by the United States Air Force began and was followed early in March by the land-ing of American marines at Danang, the war in the

South entered a new phase and for a period of four years became to all intents and purposes an American war. I have dealt elsewhere with the reasons for the American failure in South Vietnam.* Briefly, they were an obscurity of aim, a failure of strategy and a lack of control. It was never clearly understood by the American Administration, and certainly not by the army, that the whole American effort, civilian and military, had to be directed towards the establishment of a viable and stable South Vietnamese Government and State, i.e. the creation of an acceptable alternative political solution to reunification with North Vietnam under a communist government.

Instead, through the bombing of the North and a war of attrition within the South, the whole effort was directed to the military defeat of the Vietcong and of the North Vietnamese divisions infiltrated into South Vietnam. Even if such a military defeat had been possible, it would not have achieved victory without the political solution. It is just possible that a similar situation might have been reached to that which prevailed in Algeria in 1960. Even that was not reached because North Vietnam, with all the advantages of terrain and of the Vietcong organisation within the South, could retain the initiative and dictate the pace of the fighting in such a way as to impose unacceptable costs on the United States in terms of casualties, taxation and dissent which led inexorably to the erosion of American will. The costs, and especially the dissent, prompted the offer of negotiations by the United States and the search for a

* No Exit from Vietnam (Chatto and Windus, London, and David McKay, New York, 1968).

negotiated settlement. It can, therefore, be said that the bombing of North Vietnam brought the United States, not Hanoi, to the conference table. The offer of negotiations itself meant that the United States was prepared to settle for less than victory at the expense of South Vietnam. This message soon became clear both to Hanoi and to those in the South struggling to maintain their independence. When the full bombing halt was announced by President Johnson towards the end of 1968, all that it became necessary for Hanoi to do was to continue fighting "unremittingly", state her terms for victory, and then sit out the negotiations without making any concession.

During the first stage of the war Russia was in the enviable position, as co-chairman of the Geneva Conference, of being able to watch North Vietnam's successful conduct of revolutionary war without herself becoming involved other than by providing limited political, military and economic support. In spite of the 1962 majority report of the International Control Commission, which condemned North Vietnam's aggression and the consequential breaches of the Geneva Agreement by the United States and South Vietnam (it should be remembered that the United States did not exceed the permitted level of just under 700 military advisers until the end of 1961), Russia was able to protect her small ally by blocking any move to reconvene the Geneva Conference. In 1965, however, the situation was drastically changed when the first bombing raids were carried out in February on North Vietnam at the very moment when Premier Kosygin was visiting Hanoi. It may have been President Johnson's intention to show that South East Asia was an American sphere of influence and to warn the Russians off. If so, it failed. The bombing and the subsequent deployment of American combat troops in South Vietnam committed Russia to a great increase in Soviet and Eastern bloc military and economic assistance. Only Russia could supply the sophisticated anti-aircraft equipment required for the defence of North Vietnam together with trucks, fuel and other war supplies necessary to conduct the war at a much higher level of intensity at a time when Hanoi's own output was being drastically reduced by the bombing raids. From 1965 to 1969 the cost of the war to Russia greatly increased, although it was still low as compared with the United States.

Further embarrassment was caused by the need to transport many of the supplies across China and by the closure of the Suez Canal after the Six-Day war in 1967. Together with the cost, estimated to be about a billion dollars a year, the risk also increased with the possibility of a direct confrontation with the United States. However, both sides well understood the need for restraint. For example, the United States took great care not to risk the bombing or mining of Russian shipping in Haiphong harbour, and the Russians on their side did not arm the North Vietnamese with modern weapons which might have threatened either the US Fleet in the Gulf of Tonkin or American air activity in South Vietnam. Although much criticised in the communist world, particularly by China, for not reacting more directly in defence of an ally, Russia could console herself in the knowledge that the war was going well and that American strategy was itself contributing to an American defeat. There was just no need for Russia to become further involved, other than by supplying the most modern small-arms and rockets for the Tet offensive at the end of January 1968. Russia may have been a super-power but she was not yet a global power and, at this range, both the risk and the cost had to be kept to an acceptable level.

China likewise showed extreme caution. The 1965 statement by Lin Piao, to which reference has already been made, contained a major section directed at North Vietnam preaching the need for self-reliance. In spite of her vociferous attacks on United States imperialism and Russian revisionism, China herself had no desire to get directly involved in the war, particularly after she herself was being rent asunder by the Cultural Revolution. Her support and assistance continued and was even extended by the provision of labour for the repair of bomb damage to North Vietnamese road and rail communications. Hanoi was warned by China both against "adventurism", which might have provoked an American ground attack on the North, thereby compelling China to intervene as in North Korea, and against "capitulationism", that is a negotiated settlement which might end the war short of a humiliating defeat for the United States.

It was on the question of negotiations that Russian and Chinese strategy with regard to Vietnam diverged. It was the Chinese view of the war that, if North Vietnam continued the strategy of protracted war, thereby keeping American costs unacceptably high for an indefinite period, the will of the American "paper tiger" would steadily erode to the point where it would in turn cause the will of the South Vietnamese to collapse. This might then create such a chaotic situation within the South, with all government control lost, that the United States could be faced not with withdrawal but with a messy and ignominious extrication operation more or less across the beaches. Such a debâcle would destroy Western influence in Asia for ever and replace it by that of China herself (as well as having very serious repercussions elsewhere in Europe and the Third World). Such an outcome would restore China as "the central kingdom", with her position in southern Asia supreme and unassailable and her theories on revolution and revolutionary war fully vindicated.

It is this prospect of Chinese hegemony in Asia, and leadership of the communist world which might follow such a victory, which may have given Russia a reason for providing the United States with a slightly more dignified exit. Not even Hanoi could be entirely happy about such an outcome. She has been noticeably careful to maintain a balance between Russian and Chinese support in order to secure a more independent position for herself in the future. She is not fighting to restore Chinese suzerainty. One of the only advantages accruing from the United States bombing of the North was an increase of Russian influence in Hanoi, because Russia alone could provide the anti-aircraft defence. This influence has enabled Russia to advocate a smoother ending of the Vietnam war through a negotiated American withdrawal, thereby securing a North Vietnamese victory without quite such a shameful defeat for the

United States, under which most of the benefits would be reaped by China rather than Russia.

Revolutionary war as an instrument of policy is only acceptable to Russia provided that it can be controlled in the Russian interest and does not deflect her effort from other important areas. She had a lot on her plate in 1969: re-establishing orthodox communist control in Czechoslovakia and maintaining the security of her European front; restoring faith in Arab nationalist countries and extending her influence in Africa; penetrating the Indian Ocean and improving her diplomatic influence both in India and South East Asia; competing with China for communist leadership and maintaining security on her eastern frontier; competing with the United States in space and securing the defence of the Soviet base in the light of further missile and anti-missile development. All these were good reasons for keeping the Vietnam war damped down and for seeking a solution which would still secure a North Vietnamese victory without upsetting the balance of power in China's favour or in such a way that future conflicts might become unmanageable. They have prompted Russia to seek an end to the Vietnam war through a negotiated American withdrawal, which would give North Vietnam victory, relieve Russia of an expensive enterprise, thoroughly discredit the United States and thwart China.

The Tet offensive having unseated President Johnson, his successor President Nixon was left with only two unpleasant options in 1969. The first was to continue the war at a lower tempo by switching to a more sensible long-haul low-cost strategy. This would take time to compel an honourable settlement which would preserve the independence of South Vietnam and any chance of a non-communist government there. By the autumn of 1969 there were indications that within South Vietnam this strategy was to a certain extent being followed, with the result that there was an improvement in the situation on the ground and a reduction in costs as compared with 1968. Moreover Hanoi, other than sitting it out in Paris and insisting on a unilateral American withdrawal, while still conducting protracted war "unremittingly" in South Vietnam, had no new shot left in her locker, except for a possible diversion in Laos, which might provoke a hardening reaction within the United States. It was an ironic feature of the situation that, if President Nixon could have said that the United States was prepared to stay for as long as was necessary with whatever was necessary, Hanoi might have been compelled to make concessions and seek an honourable settlement (or just fade away). As it was, he could only announce further troop reductions.*

The other option was, of course, defeat, either intentional by selling out or unintentional through sustained domestic pressure in an uncomprehending democracy and a continuing process of erosion which would eventually cause a collapse in South Vietnam. A sell-out through a straight unilateral withdrawal was clearly ruled out by President Nixon and, as 1969 progressed, an unintentional defeat became the more likely of these two. The President was caught between Scylla (the six-headed monster of American dissent) and Charybdis (the whirlpool of the South Vietnamese political situation) and was being forced

* This was before his dramatic speech of 3 November.

to steer not between them but within reach of both. It would be no consolation to him, if he foundered on either, that he had merely lost President Johnson's unpopular war, because such a disaster would be likely to render all constructive future American policies, both domestic and foreign, completely sterile.

It is a fallacy to suppose that the funds and energy devoted to Vietnam would automatically be diverted to solving domestic problems or to supporting foreign policy in other areas including Europe. When a country suffers a humiliating defeat it retreats, if nothing else, to lick its wounds. Positive and constructive policies can only be carried out by a country which has all the dynamic thrust of faith in the future and of confidence in itself. The likely outcome, therefore, of defeat is that the United States would cease to be a global power and would in the end be compelled to become instead a very super nuclear power.

8

No More Vietnams

FOR THE last twenty-five years Russia's two policy
aims, communist domination of the world and the
defence of the Soviet base, have remained constant.
Her strategy has been flexible and the instruments of
policy, of which revolutionary war is one, have been
varied. It would be safe to assume that there will be
no change during the 1970s although the pattern of
conflict itself may alter. If these two policy aims are
to be successful it must be Russia's first general intention to reduce American influence, and above all
the American presence, in the European-Asian land
mass, if not to remove them altogether. This will require an easing of tension in Europe and a greater
Russian penetration of the Middle East, Indian Ocean
and South East Asia, together with an increased
mobility for Russian forces by both air and sea. There
is every indication that Russia is now moving from
the position of being a super nuclear power into one
of being also a global power.

In Europe this suggests that it will be Russian
policy to maintain the integrity of the Eastern bloc
under the Moscow party leadership and of the Warsaw Pact under Russian military leadership, while
attempting to weaken NATO by splitting Europe
from the United States and to outflank it through the
Mediterranean and North Africa. Through united
front tactics it will also be her intention to keep
individual European countries weak, divided and
indecisive, to prevent united action or any form of
European union and to encourage a European withdrawal from international involvement, partly as a
further means of isolating the United States.

In what might be called the buffer States such as

Greece, Turkey, Iran, Pakistan, India, Burma, Indonesia and Japan, all of which are geographically, economically or demographically important, it will be Russia's intention to encourage a shift of alignment away from the West towards neutralism or from neutralism closer to the bloc. The prospect of any outright aggression in these areas is remote because that might result in confrontation. Moreover, in most of these countries communism as a political or economic solution has little appeal and it is likely that united front tactics and subversion will be used to promote and exploit internal conflicts and contradictions as the opportunity occurs. Revolutionary war is also an unlikely instrument because in none of the countries is there an adequate cause on which to build up the necessary underground organisation for such a war. Moreover Russia cannot wish to become bogged down in a protracted war which might at some point escalate to confrontation. One possible exception, however, is India where in certain areas the communist party already has a firm hold on large sections of the population. For years the "agrarian crisis", mixed with student and industrial unrest, has been maturing rapidly, particularly in West Bengal, where loss of government control in the countryside was spotlighted by the Naxalbari incident* in 1967. All the ingredients for revolutionary war are present and the party, in this context under Chinese influence, is correctly directing its terror attacks, not against landlords, but against smallholders and agricultural labourers who must first be intimidated into

* See *Bengal—the Communist Challenge*, by C. R. Irani (Lalvani Publishing House).

joining the revolutionary movement to provide its rural base. Russia and China in rival competition both appreciate the vital importance of India, if not economically, at least geographically and demographically.

In the Third World we have already seen how Russia has to a certain extent solved her dilemma between the support of nationalism and the support of revolutionary forces by directing the latter against outside targets. The important areas are the Middle East and South East Asia. The former is the stepping-stone to north and east Africa, the Persian Gulf and the Indian Ocean. As yet Russia has no security of presence and tenure. Even the Egyptians in 1969, who with one hand have been taking Russian economic and military aid for years, are still with the other purging the left-wing forces in the country which might put Egypt irrevocably into the Russian camp. But the general trend in many countries is going gradually Russia's way. Until her position is more secure, Russia will not wish to become involved too actively in any revolutionary war in Africa and certainly not beyond that in Latin America. In these areas the pot can be allowed to simmer.

South East Asia, however, is doubly important to Russia. It is not a question only of eliminating American (and Western) influence from the area but of substituting Russian rather than Chinese influence in its place. In furtherance of her policy aim of securing the Soviet base Russia has largely succeeded on her European front and her main problem at the present time is stabilisation on her far Eastern front facing China. Russia, too, needs to contain China.

South East Asia is an area in which Russia has a long way to go and where she suffered one of her greatest defeats in the fall of Sukarno and the subsequent masscacre of the Indonesian Communist Party. (It is not often recognised, as Indonesian generals now admit, that they were able to take this drastic action precisely because the United States was standing in Vietnam, thereby covering them from any possible response by the communist powers.) If the communist party had succeeded in Indonesia, it would only have been Russia, not China, who could have secured the revolution and provided the necessary political, military and economic support. That having failed, Russia's new port of entry to the area has now become North Vietnam. In the early stages of the Vietnam war Russian support for Hanoi was limited. When the American bombing of the North started in 1965, Russia became more directly involved through the supply of fighters and weapons for anti-aircraft defence. Since 1967, however, Hanoi has become more and more dependent on Russia rather than China both for economic support and for military equipment. Nearly all the North Vietnamese forces fighting in the South are now equipped with Russian weapons from AK 47s to rockets. The Chinese labour force, which was required to repair the bomb damage to North Vietnam's communications, has as a result of the bombing halt now been withdrawn. While Ho Chi Minh was still alive, North Vietnam was probably able to maintain a fairly independent position with a balance of support from the two communist powers, but the indications are that Russian influence is now becoming predominant.

This brings one back to the dispute between Russia and China, which is partly traditional and partly doctrinal. Historically, more than any other Western power Russia has encroached on China. This continued, as we have seen in Chapter IV, into the Stalin period after World War II. A strong united China, even a communist one, is a threat to the security of the Soviet base. (This makes a nonsense of the claim that communism is the road to world peace —it is only necessary to compare the situation on the Russian-Chinese frontier with that, for example, on the American-Canadian border.) While China after 1950 was economically dependent on Russia and her communist party subservient to Moscow, all was well, but China was not prepared to accept the doctrine of "limited sovereignty" and roundly condemned it over Czechoslovakia in 1968. The split on doctrine has developed inevitably into a dispute for world communist leadership. Basically this boils down to a Russian desire to have communist parties, whether in power or not, which are controllable and reliable instruments of Russian policy. Russia wishes to avoid premature situations where, at long range or high risk, she may have to support communist parties which have risen to power or, worse still, to rescue them when threatened. There is a danger for Russia if North Korea, North Vietnam or Cuba, or any other communist State which may arise, become too independent and too adventurous. In the event of failure, it is Russia who would have to rescue. There is one point that Russia understands only too well, that the liberation of any country which has been under communist rule for any period of time would spell the doom of the whole system. The relief from tyranny and the subsequent economic recovery would beam such a message into the communist bloc that it might prove irresistible.

The present Chinese leadership, on the other hand, as we have seen from Mao Tse-tung's own experience in 1948, does not place the risk so high and believes in less controllable conflict and the encouragement of revolution and revolutionary war wherever and whenever opportunity offers. There is much less risk in this for China than there is for Russia. In the last resort, if she got into real trouble, she, too, might have to be rescued by Russia. She is therefore in a position to force the pace and to a certain extent to drag Russia along with her. Moreover, she herself lacks the capability, except in her immediate vicinity, to become directly involved, particularly in any military capacity. Even in her own vicinity, she has been extremely cautious in the military sense and with regard to North Vietnam for example, has preached the need for self-reliance. What concerns Russia is that China's activist policy could lead to a situation where Russia, not China, would have to pick up the pieces. The doctrine of limited sovereignty must therefore be applied to China too, so that she is both physically and ideologically contained.

It is for this reason that Russia would like to extend her influence to China's southern flank. Russia, however, needs more time to extend her penetration and secure her foothold. Provided that the United States in the end loses in South Vietnam, Russia is in no immediate hurry to see an end to the war. Quite apart from all the other benefits of an American involvement, such as an erosion of American moral authority and the exposure of her military impotence, Russia is in no position to fill the vacuum which would arise in South East Asia from an immediate American exit. She has only just advanced her proposal for regional security in the area, the intention of which is not only to keep the West out but, in spite of the influence of history and geography which in the end may prove decisive, to keep China out as well.

China, on the other hand, would like to see North Vietnam achieve a quick victory as a means of securing her own southern flank while she is engaged in a dispute with Russia on her northern and western borders. In the longer term, such a victory, with the expulsion of the United States and the retreat of Britain from East of Suez, would re-open South East Asia as her sphere of influence. One of the great myths arising from comment on the Vietnam war has been that the Chinese and Vietnamese are traditional enemies and that Vietnamese history represents a millennium of trying to throw off the Chinese yoke. In fact, past Chinese military intervention in Vietnam has nearly always been in support of one side or the other in an internal Vietnamese rebellion. China, as the suzerain power, was invited to intervene either by a threatened dynasty or by an ambitious rebel. The Chinese aim has always been to secure a friendly government (as with Russia in Poland) on her southern front. Relations with Vietnam were therefore a matter of domestic policy rather than of foreign policy. The Vietnamese attitude to China has been beautifully summed up in the lines:

> Prostrate upon the ground, the Vietnamese monarch petitions the Son of Heaven, "I hope that Your Majesty will deign to show me pity; I am no more than a tiny tributary of Your Empire and my strongest desire is to be sprinkled by the rain of Your Generosity."

With the departure of the French, Vietnam has reverted to its traditional position and China is again exercising her suzerainty to support one side against the other. It is the South Vietnamese who are trying to throw off the yoke by keeping the Chinese out.

South East Asia remains therefore not only an area of dispute between East and West but also between Russia and China for the succession. As her major instrument of policy in this respect, China is committed to revolutionary war, supported in the background by the locust-like threat of her enormous field armies and in the forefront, particularly in Laos, Cambodia and north east Thailand, by the clandestine jungle-covered presence or threat of North Vietnamese regular divisions. On two grounds Russia must be apprehensive about a successful Chinese expansionist policy. First it would lend great weight to the Chinese claim for communist leadership—that Mao is right in his analysis and that Moscow party leaders are too cautious. Secondly, such a policy contains high risks and, because of the possible rapidity of its success, could lead to confrontation between East and West, compelling Russia to make a stand in an area where she is not yet ready for it. It may well be that Russian provocation, or readiness to be provoked, on her borders with China is partly to distract China and divert her forces from any adventure in South East Asia which might spill over into India, and even further afield, and alert the West.

The containment of China both physically and ideologically, i.e. the imposition of "limited sovereignty", is essential if Russia is to retain control in achieving her general goal of eliminating American influence from the European-Asian land mass and substituting her own. This control is necessary if Russia is to develop her strategy of gradual penetration, low-level conflict and the avoidance of confrontation. For this strategy to be successful, Russia needs to keep the West confused and reluctant to become involved and to isolate the United States. There are many who will view a period of low-level conflict with optimism as an era of negotiation rather than confrontation. There may be a prospect for negotiations in the nuclear, space, consular, cultural, commercial or aviation fields because these will provide an aura of detente which will help to add to the confusion. The more rugged the track leading to any such agreements, the greater will be the sense of achievement and relief if settlements are reached. But an atmosphere of illusion will be created because none of these subjects is relevant to the real field of conflict—which is people.

Whatever limitations may be placed on the development of MIRVs (Multiple Independently-targeted Re-entry Vehicles) and ABM (Anti-Ballistic Missile) systems, it can be assumed that Russia will accept no limitation on conventional forces and the means of deploying them. It is, moreover, hard to see successful negotiations in the present areas of conflict such as the Middle East, Vietnam, Laos, Kashmir, Biafra or southern Africa. These are areas where the basic right of people to exist and determine their own future in one form or another is being decided. In accordance with Marxist-Leninist teaching a communist does not regard these forms of conflict as necessarily evil. They are instead a valuable opportunity for progress. To communists, as compared with liberal Western democrats, stability and the ending of conflict are not self-evident or desirable goals. What, therefore, Russia will prefer in the 1970s is managed instability within the illusion of a detente. Provided that confrontation can be avoided, such low-level conflicts will be promoted.

That this strategy has every chance of being successful is reinforced by a great many of the political, economic and social trends apparent in the world today. The economic gap between the developed and the underdeveloped world is continually widening. The rich countries get richer and most of the poor poorer. This also applies domestically within certain countries. One reason for the widening gap is the population explosion, which reduces or eliminates any progress in increasing the standard of living. While there may not be an overall food shortage in the world, the problem of its distribution is still not solved so that many people are living at or below starvation level. A point not often realised is that these populations are now armed, not just with sticks and stones, effective though these may be in low-level forms of conflict, but with guns. For example, a rough estimate of the total strength of the regular armed forces in the territories of the British

Empire and Commonwealth at the beginning of 1939, when a world war was about to start but before mobilization, as compared with the total strength in the same territories thirty years later in 1969, shows an increase of approximately 3½ to 1 (in spite of a decrease in the United Kingdom). Admittedly this figure is inflated by an enormous increase in India and Pakistan to nearly one and a half million men under arms. It is a sobering thought that in terms of soldiers no country in Europe can match the two halves of either Korea or Vietnam. The size of forces, for which arms and equipment are made readily available far more by the communist bloc than the West, is of course one reason for the widening economic gap. At the same time, in ex-colonial territories, the inspiration of independence has faded while the fruits of colonialism have been devoured or allowed to rot. The panacea of socialism and neutralism has failed to meet the aspirations of the people for a higher standard of living or a stable future, with the result that in some countries there is now disillusion amounting almost to despair. This is good "terrain" for a communist party, not because communism is attractive as a political philosophy, but because it offers an escape from uncertainty and a semblance of order, for which the loss of freedom seems a small price to pay.

Just as the citizen who witnesses an accident or a crime is reluctant to come forward, in order to avoid involvement with the police and the courts, so with countries there is a growing reluctance to become involved in any international issue which requires sides to be taken, particularly if it means that a

victim may have to be supported. Neutralism now
justifies an amoral attitude on controversial issues
which neutrality in war never did. General Maxwell
Taylor* has rightly divided the world into "trouble-
makers, victims and bystanders". For those who have
to cope with the first, the victims may be frustrating
but the bystanders are the most exasperating. The
dominating factor in the bystanders' position is
undoubtedly fear. The horror of nuclear war is well
understood, not least by those who could wage it and
bring about their own obliteration. In this context
fear is the enemy which alone could lead to a holo-
caust. In so far as it induces people not to take a stand
on any issue and to reconcile themselves to one
limited defeat after another, fear can lead to a situation where in a final stand only the use of nuclear
weapons would suffice. Man has not yet thrown
away any of his tools.† He has to learn to control
and live with them without fear if the human race
is to survive.

The promotion of revolution and revolutionary
war in the last twenty-five years is partly to blame
for the present wave of violence in international
affairs and domestic politics. The mere fact that some
revolutionary wars have been successful has implied
that violence pays and that any man with a cause
has a right to a gun. A central issue of our time is the
claim of the minority not to be ruled by the majority.
The whole concept of democracy is at stake. The core

* Former Chairman of the US Joint Chiefs of Staff.

† Although President Nixon, in November 1969, announced the forthcoming destruction of germ weapons in
the United States.

of the problem is, on one side, the manner in which the majority deals equitably with the minority without using the excuse of democracy to ride roughshod over it and, on the other, the acceptance by the minority of majority rule without claiming the right to secede. For those who wish to rebel against authority, whether it be world order or internal law and order, the techniques of revolutionary war, which are designed to bring a minority to power, have great attraction and much to offer. Even in a well ordered society, the promotion of a cause, the build-up of an organisation and the projection of legitimate debate into action of a guerrilla warfare type can soon lead from comparatively harmless sit-ins to uncontrollable riots and demonstrations. If a communist party has any expertise at all, it is in exploiting such opportunities to further its own political aims. Communists well understand that, in a society where traditional values of behaviour are weakening, the numbers of those who can be manipulated automatically rises. This then leads to a situation where the moderate centre in any society or country begins to erode and political forces tend to polarise towards the extremes. The road to dictatorship is then open.

The revolutionary war in Vietnam has played a prominent role in developing these social and political trends, and its exposure to the TV cameras of the world has created the greatest confusion. There are some who are impressed by the idealism, nobility and gallantry displayed by many of the revolutionaries in what would appear to be an unequal struggle against forces employing all the modern gadgetry of war. It is indeed one of the great tragedies of revolutionary war that it does produce such heroes. They are its martyrs. If they do not die in battle, they become the first victims of the subsequent purges when tyranny is imposed. Others are duped by the deceptive manoeuvres (such as the winding-up of the Indo-Chinese Communist Party in 1945, the establishment of the National Liberation Front and its subsequent elevation to provisional government status), by the bland phraseology of the manifestos (sometimes modelled on the American Declaration of Independence but always unexceptionable) and by the propaganda with its double standards and emotive words which bear no relation to reality. All this can lead to the simplistic view that, because the Vietcong have been so successful in their struggle, therefore they must be right. That is the stuff of which Quislings are made.

There are some who will require standards of perfection from threatened governments which they do not expect from their own. There can be more arrogance in liberalism than there is in power. There is a great deal of difference between a threatened government and its people fighting for national survival and a Western power supporting them and fighting for a principle (the Truman Doctrine). The conflict for each of them is at a totally different level —for one unlimited and for the other limited. Different standards must inevitably apply. It should not be surprising therefore that those fighting for national survival employ all those measures from censorship to detention which Western powers themselves apply when they are fighting for survival.

There is also a strong Anglo-Saxon prejudice against military governments. It is over a hundred years since a general has been Prime Minister of the United Kingdom, though less than ten in the United States. It is not realised that in many countries, particularly those with large armed forces, most of the talent, in terms of administrative efficiency, is in the army and that in such societies generals are just as much politicians as soldiers. They are likely to have, in addition to their military power base, as much of a civilian power base as any civilian politician. In times of stress and threat there will always be a preference for governments which are likely to be more effective and less inclined to dither.

Then there are the way-out arguments like: "Why should Americans die to keep President Thieu in power?" Many in fact died before President Thieu was ever heard of. If the war is being fought for anyone, apart from a principle, it is being fought for the South Vietnamese people. It is a stupefying thought that Americans died in World War II to keep Stalin and Churchill in power. If that was the case, they only half succeeded—and in the wrong half at that!

In any conflict there will be a labyrinth of false trails and scents. Those which are attractive to articulate liberal opinion will be enthusiastically followed. In any hundred people advancing land reform as the basic problem in South Vietnam, there is hardly one who, if asked, could describe the present system of land tenure. There is now some current research which has reached the startling conclusion that, in those areas where there has been least reform (i.e. where the worse forms of tenant-landlord relationship still remain), the Vietcong have made least headway.* Land and land administration are certainly important issues but they are not necessarily relevant to the outcome of the war in a country where, as yet, there is no great land shortage. No one has yet been able to explain why, if ownership of his own land is the issue, any peasant would support a cause which offers collectivisation as the solution. (The peasant in South Vietnam is well aware of what happened in North Vietnam after 1954 leading to the revolts in Thanh Hoa and Nghe An provinces in 1956.) It has been suggested† that collectivisation and communes in an agricultural peasant subsistence society are a less radical form of change from the traditional society than individualism and a free market economy, and are therefore the more easily swallowed, and that the idea of a plural economic and political society is too remote from a peasant's experience and therefore beyond his imagination. This could be true of some remote communities (for example, Laos) but, in my view, not in those with surplus crops for export, which have been subjected to a strong Western trading influence for more than fifty years. In fact a free market economy has been traditional in South Vietnam for centuries, which partly accounts for the trouble the North is now experiencing when the collectivisation programme was relaxed during the bombing to allow the peasants of North Vietnam to cultivate

* See note on page 14.

† By Dr Coral Bell (in an article in the *International Journal*, Toronto, of Summer 1968).

private plots which they are now reluctant to give up.

There has also been a great reluctance to face up to the "domino theory". Because it suggests such unpleasant consequences of an American defeat in Vietnam, much effort has been devoted to arguments attempting to disprove it. These have been greedily devoured by those who want to ignore the consequences. The answer is to ask the dominoes. Tunku Abdul Rahman of Malaysia has always regarded South Vietnam as his "front line" (his very words to me in 1961), while Mr Lee Kuan Yew of Singapore has constantly repeated the same theme using the words: "Nothing would be more disastrous than to see South Vietnam just erode away and become absorbed into the communist group. It would telescope the time left to the rest of us. If people start believing that non-communist Asia will be lost eventually to communist Asia, then everybody will make his adjustment accordingly." It is for this very reason that both the Thai and Philippine governments have committed troops in support of South Vietnam. The people of South East Asia understand what the war is about as do others further afield. Is it just a coincidence that, when America is "standing in Vietnam", the people of the Eastern bloc should be so receptive to Western ideas and even prepared to act on them? Only if the West is prepared to make a stand will the hopes of all those peoples now subject to communist tyranny be kept alive.

Now in the summer of 1969, after twenty-five years of almost continual revolutionary wars, there seems

NO MORE VIETNAMS / 155

less rather than more understanding of their nature,
purpose and course than there was during the early
cold war period. Few Americans realise that, while the
Tet offensive of 1968 was a traumatic victory for
Hanoi in the United States, it was, when coupled
with the later failure of the offensives in May and
August of that year, a defeat in South Vietnam,
from which they have not yet recovered. Apart from
the losses, the velvet glove was removed and the
South Vietnamese will not forget the slaughter in
Hué. It is only necessary to look back to March,
1968, when the soldiers were asking for 200,000
more troops and the airmen were preparing a massive
bombing assault on the North as the weather improved. Neither of these occurred and, by the
autumn of 1969, 60,000 American troops were being
withdrawn without any sign of South Vietnam
falling apart. An improved performance by the South
Vietnamese Government, coupled with a reduced
capacity on the part of the North Vietnamese and
Vietcong, as a result of the failure to achieve victory
in 1968, has been slowly tipping the scales. It is not
an improvement that would be noticed by the critics.
Improvement was not apparent to the critics in
Malaya, when even the late Dr Victor Purcell, with
thirty years' experience of South East Asia, could
write in 1953:

Unfortunately, while the military campaign to
date shows no signs of reaching a successful conclusion, the measures taken by General Templer
to bring Malaya further on the road towards self-
government or to raise the standard of living of

the people have not been impressive enough to rally the support of the people as a whole on the side of the Government. . . . The departure of General Templer [in the following year], if the British people can be made aware of the facts, should be the signal for a complete re-consideration of British policy and attitudes.

But within that year, before the General left in 1954, the war was won and, by 1955, it was the communists who were asking for negotiations. By 1957, Malaya, under Tunku Abdul Rahman with an overwhelming elected majority, was independent.

Many believed that the opening of substantive negotiations in Paris, after President Johnson had halted the bombing of North Vietnam and after the shape of the table had been agreed, would lead to the end of the Vietnam war within a few months and to a settlement at the conference table. The argument was that, because neither side could win a military victory, therefore there was a stalemate and therefore there must be a negotiated settlement. It was still not appreciated that revolutionary wars must result in a decision one way or the other and that a settlement, if such it could be called, would only reflect victory for one side or the other. Either South Vietnam would be preserved as an independent state or absorbed, perhaps after a short transitional period before reunification, by the communist Hanoi government.

By a process of argument based entirely on wishful thinking and illusion it was (and is still) assumed that the United States could end the war at will and some fanciful solutions were proposed. Some favoured a coalition to which neither North nor South would agree. The North contended that the National Liberation Front was already a coalition, while the South would offer only free elections under international supervision which the Vietcong knew they would lose. Even if a coalition between the Saigon Government and the NLF was feasible, it would utterly demoralise the non-communist forces in the South and, by making the communist party legal, would enable it to continue subversion and terror with impunity. Communists are not interested in sharing power with other parties. As in Czechoslovakia in 1948, a coalition would lead inevitably to an eventual communist take-over.

A few advocated a standstill cease-fire in place thus recommending a form of partition of territory without recognising that there are no clear cut divisions, with many areas still disputed on which no agreement could be reached. Nor could Hanoi and the NLF readily agree to such a plan. They do not hold a single town and are not interested in holding outlying villages, swamps and jungle. As solutions a coalition or a standstill cease-fire are only of interest because their proposers are prepared to do unto others what they are not prepared to do unto themselves. No Democratic contender for the Presidency offered a seat in his Cabinet to the "Black Power" movement and no American politician has yet suggested a standstill in the ghetto with "Black Power" as a separate authority in legal control.

Others have suggested early target dates for the withdrawal of all American combat troops (a partial sell-out) but leaving behind up to 100,000 men in non-combat units to provide logistic and other support for the South Vietnamese. (It ought to be clear by now that revolutionary wars cannot be fought to target dates by either side.) No President of the United States, responsible as Commander-in-Chief for the lives of his men, could possibly commit a force of that size and constitution to such circumstances without the backing of combat troops for its protection.

All the above proposals, coming as they do mainly from Democratic sources within the United States, merely show that those who originally sponsored and supported the American stand have been disenchanted by their own failure and have deserted their own cause. That the liberals are now in a state of complete intellectual disarray is one of the great successes of revolutionary war in world strategy. That a defeat in Vietnam could lead to the disruption of American society, and consequently of the Western Alliance, could make that particular revolutionary war one of the decisive wars of history.

The point is that the United States cannot now extricate herself from South Vietnam without a sell-out and without suffering a humiliating defeat which would have serious consequences internationally, both in South East Asia and the rest of the world, and domestically within the United States. Leader writers, academicians and columnists have vied with each other to propound post-Vietnam policies which have ignored these consequences, and which take no account of the fact that the outcome of the war has not yet been decided. It has been the generally

expressed view that there will be "no more Vietnams" and that the world is entering an era of
negotiation not of confrontation, leading hopefully to
co-operation between the United States and Russia in
the maintenance of world order. There is a striking
similarity of thought here with the period immediately
following World War II, when there should have been
greater prospects of co-operation following the wartime alliance. The policy and strategy of the United
States and the West in the 1970s cannot be based
on such illusions and must take into account the
hard reality of the Vietnam war and the consequences of an American defeat.

It may be true that there will be no more Vietnams.
Attempts to create another Vietnam elsewhere have
been remarkably unsuccessful. Where the terrain is
suitable for revolutionary war, the conditions do not
exist nor are the people temperamentally suited for
such a protracted type of warfare requiring great
discipline coupled with mental and physical endurance. Communism itself as a cause has no attraction
and the opportunities no longer exist for a communist party to build up the required organisation in
phase one on the patriotic cause of resistance to a
conqueror or of national independence. The pretexts
on which such wars may be fought in phases two and
three, while present in many areas, are not enough
on which to build the necessary base for revolutionary
war. Any "national liberation movements" which
do surface (possibly in India) are unlikely to achieve
the momentum, scale and tempo of those which
have been considered in this book. Revolutionary
war has been a post-war phenomenon which is likely

to subside into a lower level of conflict but to leave behind a "fall-out" which will express itself in minor revolts, sporadic guerrilla activity, urban demonstrations, riots and continuing *coups d'état*.

To say, therefore, that the United States will not become involved in another Vietnam is probably true as a matter of fact, but it is certainly unwise as a statement of policy. As the latter, it can lead to a variety of interpretations. As with Mr Dean Acheson's statement on South Korea in 1950, it can be interpreted by some, notably China, North Korea and North Vietnam, as an invitation to an active interventionist policy in Asia without fear of an American response. As explained, Russia has no more desire than the United States to become involved in another Vietnam. She has been just as hooked to North Vietnam as the United States has been to South Vietnam. She is likely to prefer a more flexible role and less expensive commitments at such extreme ranges. Besides, from the Russian point of view, if the United States is defeated, Vietnam will have served its purpose. One will have been enough.

The countries of South East Asia and elsewhere in the Third World may interpret such a statement of policy as a renunciation of the Truman Doctrine. If this leads them to believe that they will be lacking outside support when they most need it, the governments and peoples of these countries cannot be expected to make any determined stand when faced by the threat of underground subversion and covert aggression. When revolutionary forces know that they will be supported and counter-revolutionary forces think that they won't be, all the psychological advantage will lie with the former and the war will be over before it is fought.

Worst of all, such a statement will increase the reluctance of the United States to become involved at all and of the West to support her. It will merely increase the fear that any involvement could develop into another Vietnam. It has to be accepted that involvement can lead to either success or failure. Non-involvement only leads to failure, possibly a less expensive failure, but a failure none the less. The answer is to keep the options open. A declaration of intent can always be qualified by some such words as "except in exceptional circumstances". A statesman should never say "Never". If, however, the words "No more Vietnams" mean that the United States has learnt the lessons of revolutionary war and proposes to revise her strategy not her policy, then such wars would certainly cease to play such a significant part as an instrument of communist policy in the future. That, however, is not the generally accepted interpretation, and the basic trends in the East-West conflict and the social and political trends within Western society seem to be leading to a situation where there is a lack of unity in the West, an isolation of the United States, a reluctance to become involved and complete confusion on the issues. No situation could be more suited in the 1970s to a communist strategy of promoting low-level conflict and manageable turmoil within the limits required by minimum world stability. Direct confrontation with its risks of escalation and of restoring Western unity would be carefully avoided. The rules of the game, as laid down by Russia, would be that communist countries are off-limits, that the remainder are a free-for-all, and that, in any free-for-all, a communist party only has to win once. The advancement of Russia's two policy aims would under these rules gather momentum because she would have achieved a can-win can't-lose position.

The West was warned by Mr I. R. Sinai in 1964 in his book *The Challenge of Modernisation** when he wrote:

> The outstanding and irreversible fact of contemporary history, then, is that Western civilisation is now under concentrated attack on many fronts. It is being attacked not only by communist imperialism, but also harassed and blackmailed by Afro-Asian nationalism and neutralism . . . More and more the general impression is spreading that the Western countries lack that generosity of endeavour, that force of thrust and initiative, that sort of daring and faith in their own powers and that mercurial and buoyant spirit that are the true marks of a civilisation at the height of its strength and energies. Western civilisation may therefore, if this is true, as it seems to be, increasingly become a small, gravely threatened, numerical minority surrounded by millions upon millions who are either openly hostile to its ideas, beliefs and way of life or else contemptuously neutralist.

The part played by revolutionary war in this process has been magnified by the agony of Vietnam which has obscured the issue. It should in fact be as clear today as when President Truman went down

* Chatto and Windus, 1964.

to Congress in support of Greece in 1947. It was reaffirmed by President Nixon in his speech to the United Nations in September, 1969, when he said that, while America wanted to end the Vietnam war, she stood firm on only one basic principle: that the people of South Vietnam must enjoy the right to determine their own future without outside interference. In the intervening years there has been a long history of American support for countries threatened by revolutionary war, subversion or economic collapse. In Asia alone, from Afghanistan to Japan, United States aid has exceeded $30 billions. The general aim was to ensure sufficient stability so that a political choice always remained open to the peoples concerned. If that policy is now changed, the foundation of the whole structure will collapse, leading to increased violence and to the rise of those who know how to exploit violence in politics, which is exactly the situation that communist strategy is attempting to create. In such circumstances no government with any claim to a liberal or democratic base, or with any hope of developing such a base, could survive.

The argument of extremes in the United States is between those who advocate isolationism of the Fortress America type and those who would maintain a world policeman role. The answer is to find a middle course, which still supports the basic principle and allows all nations to feel secure in their independence and sovereignty. This requires, as Mr McNamara has pointed out, collective security complemented by collective development. The burden cannot be borne by the United States alone, nor can security be confined solely to weapons development or the application of military power. The problem is people with all their aspirations unfulfilled. Development, whether regional or national, in all its forms, both organisational and productive, as a means of restoring confidence in the future is the key to security.

The strategy to support this policy has already been proposed by President Nixon as one of continued limited assistance by the United States and of encouraging all countries to do it themselves. This long-haul low-cost strategy is the right approach in a period of low-level conflict offering, as it does, help when required but promoting an attitude of self-reliance, both in defence and development, which is essential if countries are to stand confidently on their own feet.

In relation to Vietnam, this approach is the whole point of the "Vietnamisation" policy. It is not just a matter of Vietnamese troops replacing American troops in the war. It means a progressive build-up of South Vietnamese capability for their future defence and development so that, in the end, they can stand on their own feet, thereby resisting outside inter-ference and giving their people the opportunity to choose their own form of government and their own way of life. As Mr Melvin Laird, the American Secretary for Defence, pointed out, this requires a stronger administration, a stronger economy, stronger military forces and stronger police for internal security. To achieve these, limited American support in all forms will still be necessary but at a steadily decreasing rate. Not only can the war in Vietnam still be won through this new strategy but, unless that strategy is first proved successful in Vietnam, it will lack all credibility for those nations of the Third World, and in Europe, which must still rely on limited American support.

It has been the tragedy of the last decade that the United States has had to stand almost alone and that the countries of Europe, which were the fount of Western civilisation, have been obsessed with their economic and social problems, thereby losing most, if not all, of their political military and moral influence. If the trends are to be reversed, so that hope and confidence in the future for all peoples in the free world and behind the iron curtain are restored, it is not enough that the United States alone should stand "a mighty woman with a torch". Europe, too, must find a role and re-light its torch.

Index